Penelope Hobhouse's
GARDEN DESIGNS

Penelope Hobhouse's
GARDEN DESIGNS

Penelope Hobhouse

in association with

Simon Johnson

HENRY HOLT AND COMPANY
NEW YORK

Henry Holt and Company, Inc.
Publishers since 1866
115 West 18th Street
New York, New York 10011

Henry Holt® is a registered trademark
of Henry Holt and Company, Inc.

Published in Canada by Fitzhenry & Whiteside
Ltd., 195 Allstate Parkway, Markham, Ontario
L3R 4T8.

Library of Congress Cataloging-in-Publication
Data is available on request.

ISBN 0-8050-4862-6

Henry Holt books are available for special
promotions and premiums.
For details contact: Director, Special Markets.

First American Edition—1997

Printed in Hong Kong

All first editions are printed on acid-free paper. ∞

10 9 8 7 6 5 4 3 2 1

HALF TITLE PAGE *The weeping willow at the
Pilkington's garden (see page 92) displays its pale
leaves in spring. A new bridge beyond the sitting
area under the wall rounds off the plans and
provides a route around the garden. Flowerbeds
still have to fill up to give a feeling of maturity.*

TITLE PAGE *In the garden just outside Detroit in
Michigan (see page 44) four separate box-edged
compartments are dominated by glazed pots.
Amsonias (Amsonia tabernaemontana) have
pale blue flowers in spring and golden foliage in
autumn. In two of the beds Lilium 'Scarlet
Emperor' comes up through the amsonia to flower
in summer; in the other two Crocosmia lucifer,
with iris-like leaves, flowers later in the summer.*

CONTENTS PAGE *At Bettiscombe (see page 149) tall
verbascums give height and architecture to the
new Gravel Garden. Herbaceous plants, although
only there in the summer, can be as important as
major shrubs in any planting scheme. The gravel,
which acts as a mulch over the soil, makes it easy
to walk and weed between the plants and prevents
compaction.*

CONTENTS

OPPOSITE *In my garden at Bettiscombe, described in more detail on pages 148-57, standard globe locusts, which define the cubic space and act as ceilings in the upper level, allow a glimpse of the Dorset countryside in which the garden is set. Under the trees the quite formal design is disguised by a profusion of plants. Steps, hidden by a froth of lime-green lady's mantle, provide links with the lower level where the Gravel Garden imitates nature.*

INTRODUCTION

Writing this book has meant revisiting gardens I have been involved with since 1986. Noting how they have developed and trying to articulate my intentions and philosophies, as well as reflecting on a decade of changes in approach and style, has been a new and thought-provoking experience.

There have also been changes in the way I work, which have broadened the scope of the more recent designs. For the last six years I have worked closely with Simon Johnson, mostly in Britain and in Europe, and with Nan Sinton, an outstanding plantswoman, in the United States. We've been lucky to work in many different countries and climates, in each new region being able to learn from local horticultural experts.

Simon has a true understanding of space manipulation; he is probably stricter than me about principles. I am older and know that a compromise often 'works'. We make a good team as he constantly reminds me not to spoil simplicity by overplanting and using complicated plant associations. I remind Simon that clients have a vision too, a vision it is our job to realise for them. Gardens are an emotive subject and sometimes we have been asked to make compromises hard to accept, but having to re-think our attitudes is another learning process, and the resulting garden actually benefits rather than loses. Of course we do not always faithfully interpret

our clients' ideas but try to guide them so that they come to appreciate wider issues: what style is appropriate to their garden, what plants will grow in the soil and climate.

Because we have studied the great designers of the past and visited many of the great gardens, we have learnt the grammar and 'tricks of the trade' at first hand. We are both experienced, almost passionate, gardeners and believe that having a feeling for plants makes us more useful designers.

The first step in designing is to get the basics right: the rules of proportion and balance. Gardens are about using space, they are 'rooms', volumes of cubic space, which relate to their surroundings. The architecture is supplied by buildings, walls, steps, and pergolas but, most importantly, by plants. Large trees frame the sky and balance with the mass of the house, hedges provide verticals and horizontal lines (as well as a background to later planting). Small trees with broad, globular or pyramidal heads act as 'ceilings' to enhance the room-like effects. Low continuous hedging frames pathways and the paths themselves, as functional as possible, combine with slopes and steps to link garden areas.

In more naturalistic gardening, a knowledge of plant habits is essential. Although proportion and balance are still important, the designer, less an architect now, becomes a painter. Here the aim is to

disguise the artificial composition with the imitation of nature and, like an artist, to compose with plants. But the composition is not static – gardens are a series of consecutive pictures, revealed as you walk through its spaces.

We adapt our layouts to the 'spirit of the place' and the owner's requirements and, once we get the basics agreed, consider the 'furnishing' plants; we step aside and what is chosen greatly depends on the owner's personal preference. Some of our clients regard our Master Plans as blueprints, surprised that, at planting time, plants are shuffled and tweaked by eye to get the best effects. We help them to understand that in garden designing there is a fourth dimension – time; time for plants to mature and establish relationships which do not appear on a two-dimensional plan.

There are many practical considerations. We take many photographs, make surveys for levels, take measurements, assess the climate and analyse the soil for acidity or alkalinity. Perhaps the most important key to success is soil preparation and eradication of perennial weeds, even importing new topsoil if necessary.

Finally, gardens should provide shade and shelter, seats for contemplation, scents and solitude, and require just the amount of maintenance to encourage relaxation because, above all, they are places to be enjoyed.

MIXED BORDERS AND A CUTTING GARDEN

In 1986 I was asked to design various areas of the La Faisanderie garden at Royaumont in the north-east of the Île de France. It was my first important assignment. I had advised friends and done quite a few one-off affairs (a day's consultancy here and there) but this was the real thing – exciting, stimulating but also very intimidating. I had no experience of running a design office and initially had no back-up, though I eventually found a student, Philip Gamble, at Cannington Horticultural College in Somerset, to help with some of the drawings. I did not even know how and what to charge.

I owed my introduction to the family who owned the garden to a very old friend, the painter Derek Hill who had given them a copy of my recently published book, *Colour in Your Garden*. It was a wonderful opportunity, and since then the family's patronage has opened many other doors for me, both in designing and in lecturing.

The gardens at Royaumont included a rhododendron wood, some hedges (in particular, an imposing one of yew, enclosing the garden to the west), a swimming pool in the centre of the lawn, some damp cold woodland, and a vegetable garden. They needed a face-lift and the main border had been emptied of plants and was ready for a new design.

The client was interested in my colour planting, and had some very definite views on what he wanted. Without really altering much of the existing layout, I was initially to make a series of 'gardens' within the garden – though in the end, I was involved in many other parts of the garden as well. He wanted a Main Border, running from north to south, against the 75m (250ft) yew hedge. This could be 3m (10ft) wide, and would be visible from the south-facing windows of the house. Near the swimming pool he wanted a flowerbed adjoining the woodland garden and rhododendron area. This was to be planted with blue and white flowers set off by plants with silvery foliage. To the north-west of the house he wanted to replace some rather unsatisfactory planting with a long walk, a cross axis of apple espaliers, an area for cutting flowers including roses (for the family's apartment in Paris as well as for the house), and a herb garden.

The soil at Royaumont is a sandy loam with a pH of 7.3-7.9. It needs heavy feeding each autumn with both manure and leaf mould to help it retain moisture. The rhododendrons have additional acid-based compost added each year. But although the soil is free-draining, Royaumont is surrounded by wetlands, and problems arise when the river occasionally overflows into the garden in winter.

Winters in Île de France have temperatures falling to -30° C (-23° F) (although more recent winters have been milder). Spring comes suddenly, with daytime temperatures shooting into the mid 20 degrees C (mid 70 degrees F), accompanied by quite severe night frosts – dangerous for newly planted young shrubs and often catching the emerging leaves of plants such as hostas, rodgersias and veratrums. Planting out of annuals and tender shrubs used as annuals is done in mid May after careful hardening off. Summers have been getting hotter in recent years, so biennials, normally sown outside in June and July, are now sown later and overwintered in cold frames.

When I began work at Royaumont, there was an old gardener in charge, but he was due to retire shortly. He gardened in a timeless traditional way (he gave me his own recipe for a hot-bed) and was a wonderfully hard worker. Work began early, at about 7 a.m. (6 in the heat of summer), with a long lunch hour at midday but no English-style tea breaks or pauses. Within a few months we found Jim Priest, then a student at the Royal Botanic Gardens at Kew, to take over when the old gardener retired. Without Jim's knowledge and taste my plans could not have been implemented and matured, and Jim has since brought his own ideas – as well as outlying neglected areas – into the garden.

In 1985 I found lots of good plants in the garden but much of the planting was haphazard and little attention had been paid

8

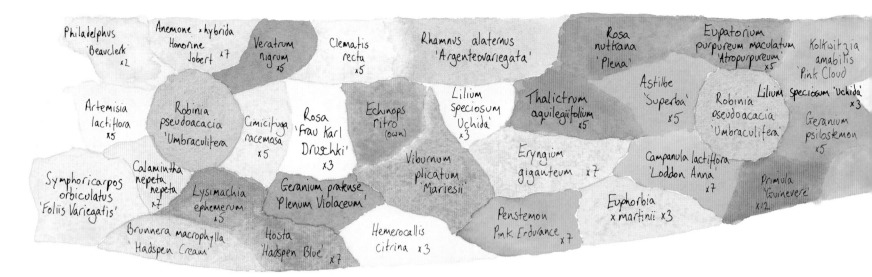

Rosa moyesii 'Geranium'

to plant association. I was surprised to see masses of white impatiens, although used here to great effect, carpeting shady areas under magnolias and other spreading shrubs. Dotted about everywhere were single groups of the variegated *Hosta undulata*, distracting the eye. I suggested moving these *en masse* to a circular bed (at that time an unsatisfactory shallow pool) in the woodland, where their white and green leaves, glowing in the shade, became an effective surprise feature. The front drive had no structured avenue-like planting and lacked drama, so we planted hedges of hornbeam (*Carpinus betulus*) to create a tunnel-like effect before emerging into the sunlit gardens near the house.

This was my first major enterprise and I was still both economical – hence finding a new purpose for the hostas – and convinced of the merits of planting 'small' rather than creating 'instant' effects by using more mature plants. I therefore proposed putting in hornbeam of less than 1m (3ft) in height, knowing that they would quickly establish and double in height in a few seasons. Many clients find two-dimensional flat plans difficult to interpret, and when planting it is important to stress the ultimate relativity of

plant sizes from the beginning. If trees and hedges are very small, they will be dwarfed at first by tall perennials, and it needs a strong imagination to visualize the eventual appearance of the garden. The designer is only a guide along the road to a common goal, and it is his or her job to stimulate and interpret the owner's vision and to bring it to realization as soon as is practicably possible. Fortunately, the client ordered tall hornbeams for the drive at Royaumont, and I received a lesson in the value of immediate structure.

The existing yew hedge made a superb background to the Main Border, which would be seen from the house throughout the year. The border was already prepared – slightly undulating, widening and narrowing, although without being in any way what Gertrude Jekyll disdainfully called 'wriggly' – and I suggested that we should develop different colour schemes along its length, which would unfold in succession for the visitor. At the north end, nearest the house, we chose pinks and sober reds as the dominant colour, set off by glossy leaves of acanthus: roses, kolkwitzia, the subtle *Viburnum sargentii* 'Onondaga', my favourite

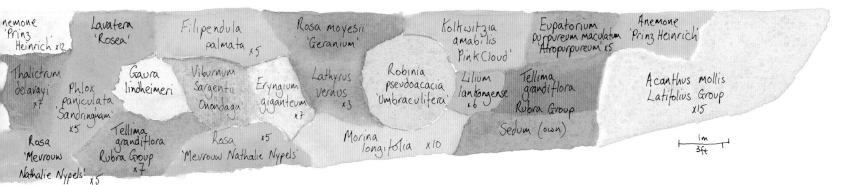

Anemone 'Prinz Heinrich' x12

Lavatera 'Rosea'

Filipendula palmata x5

Rosa moyesii 'Geranium'

Kolkwitzia amabilis 'Pink Cloud'

Eupatorium purpureum maculatum 'Atropurpureum' x5

Anemone 'Prinz Heinrich'

Thalictrum delavayi x7

Phlox paniculata 'Sandringham' x5

Gaura lindheimeri

Viburnum Sargentii 'Onondaga'

Eryngium giganteum x7

Lathyrus vernus x3

Robinia pseudoacacia 'Umbraculifera'

Lilium lankongense x6

Tellima grandiflora Rubra Group

Acanthus mollis Latifolius Group x15

Rosa 'Mevrouw Nathalie Nypels' x5

Tellima grandiflora Rubra Group x7

Rosa 'Mevrouw Nathalie Nypels' x5

Morina longifolia x10

Sedum (own)

1m / 3ft

The Main Border

dark-stemmed form of eupatorium, groups of pink lilies – all backed by autumn-flowering Japanese anemones. The shrubs would take the border through from spring to late summer. The next section consisted of creams and whites with some variegated foliage, brought to life with the hybrid musk rose 'Buff Beauty'. Further south we used blues and yellows, complementary colours which always work well together: camassias, hardy geraniums, campanulas, bright achilleas and gentle lady's mantle (*Alchemilla mollis*). The final touch was to introduce four standard globe-headed black locusts (*Robinia pseudoacacia* 'Umbraculifera') at regular intervals along the border, thus ensuring vertical height and emphasis throughout the year but also, importantly, using their formal repetition to tie the whole design together. The trees were obtained from a Dutch nursery as 1.7m (5ft 6in) standards.

The next garden, near the swimming pool, was more of a problem. Designed as a summer garden, but north-facing and backed by the rhododendron wood, it needed some sort of design feature, such as a hedge, to separate it and the woodland.

ABOVE Lilium lankongense
BELOW Morina longifolia

ABOVE Veratrum nigrum
BELOW Thalictrum aquilegifoliium

11

ABOVE Salvia patens
BELOW Artemisia ludoviciana

BELOW Hosta Sieboldiana 'Frances Williams'

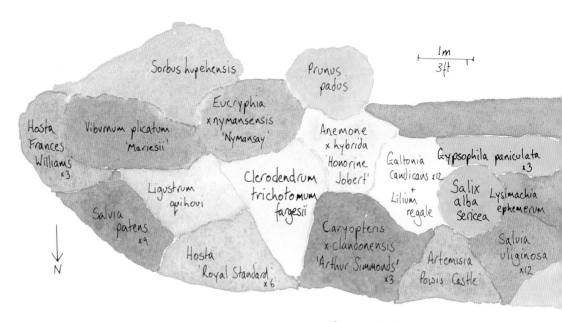

Sorbus hupehensis
Prunus padus
1m
3ft
Hosta 'Frances Williams' x3
Viburnum plicatum 'Mariesii'
Eucryphia x nymansensis 'Nymansay'
Anemone x hybrida 'Honorine Jobert'
Galtonia candicans x12 + Lilium regale
Gypsophila paniculata x3
Salix alba sericea
Lysimachia ephemerum
Ligustrum quihoui
Clerodendrum trichotomum fargesii
Salvia patens x9
Hosta 'Royal Standard' x6
Caryopteris x clandonensis 'Arthur Simmonds' x3
Artemisia 'Powis Castle'
Salvia uliginosa x12
N

Blue and Grey Border

I suggested using sea buckthorn (*Hippophae rhamnoides*) – tall, dark-stemmed, with silver foliage and orange berries in autumn – as a divider. Otherwise, the planting was primarily for colour – blue, white and silver – and of course scent. Looking for spectacular effects meant that I had to choose plants which, in the waterlogged soil, would often need to be replaced: caryopteris, blue salvias, grey-leaved artemisias, regal lilies, blue and white agapanthus. These were backed by tall willows and a clerodendrum (*Clerodendrum trichotomum* var. *fargesii*) for late summer fragrance, with shade-tolerant shrubs such as hydrangeas (*Hydrangea arborescens* – still my favourite hydrangea) and glaucous-leaved hostas at either end. Clematis and the white-flowered perennial sweet pea were grown to straggle through the sea buckthorn hedge.

In the north-west garden we designed a new east-west alley, the Long Walk, to the end of the garden. The vista was later improved by opening up woodland to reveal the countryside beyond a stream, and to frame a statue. Espalier apples flanked the walk, divided by trellis-work pillars on which scented honeysuckle (*Lonicera japonica* 'Halliana') was trained. On the cross axis old varieties of pears replaced the apples as espaliers. The beds under the espaliers were planted mainly with annuals: salvias, including clary, *Salvia patens* and *S. viridis*, tall *Nicotiana sylvestris* and the more delicate

RIGHT *At dawn the Blue and Grey Border has an ethereal quality, enhanced by the dark shadows. In late summer, blue and white agapanthus, blue salvias – both* Salvia patens *and, at the back,* S. uliginosa *– are elevated by the more solid shape and large flowerheads of the hydrangea, which have a greenish tinge. Miss Jekyll once said, 'A blue garden does not only have to have blue flowers, it just has to be beautiful.' She often used regale lilies to make her basically blue schemes more glowing. Soil preparation and incorporation of gravel and organic composts improve the drainage for some of these plants, marginally tender at Royaumont.*

Hedge of Hippophae rhamnoïdes

Prunus padus

Nicotiana sylvestris x9

standard Salix helvetica

Lathyrus latifolius 'Albus'

Clematis 'Alba Luxurians' on hoop

Hydrangea arborescens

Clematis rehderiana on hoop

Lathyrus latifolius 'Albus'

standard Salix helvetica

Nicotiana Sylvestris x9

Gypsophila paniculata

Galtonia candicans + x12

Lilium regale x12

Ligustrum quihoui

Aster x frikartii 'Mönch' x7

Salix alba sericea

Hosta 'Frances Williams' x5

Artemisia ludoviciana

Salvia Patens x9

Agapanthus (White) x5

Salvia patens x9

Artemisia ludoviciana

Salvia guaranitica

Aster x frikartii 'Mönch' x7

Caryopteris x clandonensis 'Ferndown' x3

Hebe pinguifolia 'Pagei'

Agapanthus Headbourne hybrids

Artemisia 'Powis Castle'

Agapanthus (White) x5

Agapanthus Headbourne hybrids

Hebe pinguifolia 'Pagei'

Artemisia 'Powis Castle'

N. langsdorffii, Argyranthemum 'Jamaica Primrose' and many others. Over the years Jim Priest would think of many additions. Although planned originally by me as a Cutting Garden, this area is mainly kept for display and is one of the most successful.

Further garden space lay to the north in front of the old garden frames. There I recommended massed picking beds, a paved rose garden edged with scented pinks and with a central pergola, and a herb garden with a catmint (*Nepeta* x *faassenii*) border surrounding it. Sweet peas grew on willow wigwams and a group of three mulberry trees was planted near the stream next to a tea crab (*Malus hupehensis*). At Royaumont tall trees and soaring poplars provide a country setting for the whole garden.

LEFT *A close-up of one of the espaliered apples in the Long Walk. The trees are pruned twice a year, once lightly in summer and then more severely in mid winter. Espaliered fruit, either as step-overs, with one low layer of espalier, or with two or three or more layers of branches, makes a useful divide in a garden. They allow views right across garden beds, where a solid hedge would be less appropriate.*

RIGHT *Looking south to the intersection of the apple and pear alleys, the planting is almost 'mirror image' on the four corners. Silver artemisias, verbenas and salvias are echoed on each side, between the formal fruit trees and rhythm of repeated honeysuckle. Sharp lawn edges strengthen the manicured look.*

PREVIOUS PAGES *In the Cutting Garden, behind the honeysuckle and espaliered fruit, a profusion of annuals, planted in glorious sweeps of colour, makes a meadow-like effect. These plants are grown for cutting, but there are more than enough to keep the garden looking well at the end of the season. Golden marigolds, orange helianthus and annual coneflowers (forms of rudbeckia) are mixed in with mauve-flowered verbenas and Malva sylvestris.*

OPPOSITE *The view up the garden, taken from an upper window, shows the hybrid musk roses 'Penelope' and 'Buff Beauty' in their June luxuriance, with the rose 'Mevrouw Nathalie Nypels' flowering in the lower beds. This latter, a China rose with glossy almost bronze new foliage, has a very long flowering season, especially if carefully deadheaded. The Macphersons have added the low box hedge.*

ABOVE *Shrubs and climbers effectively screen the neighbours throughout the year. In early summer, Ceanothus 'Cascade', with its almost pendulous habit, produces a mass of blue flowers in this warm London garden. The pot plants on the terrace add an extra dimension to the garden plans.*

PLANTING SCHEMES FOR A NARROW SITE

I began working on the garden at 28 Campden Hill Square for the Macphersons in 1986. The house was still being renovated. At this time I did not have a proper office but I was able to work with the architect Christopher Smallwood who did all the technical drawings required for paving, walls and steps, including the brick patterns.

I found a typical long narrow garden sloping steeply up south of the house. Modern buildings beyond the far perimeter were fortunately screened by a substantial *Catalpa bignonioides*. High walls, though not high enough, flanked the sides to provide privacy and support for climbers. There was access at the side of the house and a very useful gateway almost at the end of the garden on the west side.

The design for the new garden was very simple. Levels were adjusted to provide three distinct horizontal areas, linked by a central axis of brick steps. Wide by the house, the groundplan narrows and widens again, which tricks the eye into thinking that the garden is wider than it really is. The terrace immediately outside the kitchen and dining-room allows room for eating out and sitting, as well as for some ornamental pots. The Macphersons have added more plants in containers over the years.

The terrace is paved with terracotta tiles, a follow-through from the kitchen, but brick steps and landings, constructed with London stock to match the existing walls, carry the eye to the top of the garden. From the terrace the view narrows up five shallow steps to a landing with rich planting; artemisia, catmint and verbenas sprawling over the brick pathway. Further steps lead to an open, nearly circular lawn, beyond which a slightly raised platform draws the eye to a focal point, an ornament placed in front of the catalpa set in a sea of periwinkle at the end of the garden. Square trelliswork panels on top of the walls add height and privacy; on these twining climbers scramble and wall shrubs are tied in.

From the beginning I was influenced by the simple, almost classical, taste of Hilary and Donald Macpherson. They wanted a comfortable garden for living in and for entertaining; it was to be a background and setting for their lives. The choice of plants was important, with an emphasis on summer colours and pastel tints – pink roses such as 'Mevrouw Nathalie Nypels' mingling with silvery foliage – rather than vivid eye-catching reds or oranges.

I knew at once that the garden would be looked after, and probably improved over the years, and I was right. It is a designer's nightmare to have no faith in the garden's future, but ten years later the garden, with lots of Macpherson touches, is immaculate. Of course some of the small trees and larger

Hydrangea anomala petiolaris

Gate

Lonicera etrusca

Clematis 'Huldine'

Clematis 'Royal Velours'

Robinia pseudoacacia Frisia

Rhamnus alaternus 'Argenteovariegata'

Camellia x williamsii 'J C Williams'

Camellia sasanqua

Viburnum x burkwoodii

Hydrangea quercifolia

Astilbe rivularis x3

Philadelphus coronarius 'Aureus'

Camellia x williamsii 'Donation'

Prunus sargentii underplanted with Scilla siberica Alchemilla mollis

Paeonia 'Bowl of Beauty'

Paeonia

Erythronium revolutum

Hosta 'Hadspen Blue' x5

Mahonia 'Undulata'

Helleborus x sternii

Path

Osmanthus delavayi

Gillenia trifoliata x3

Hedera colchica 'Sulphur Heart'

Cyclamen hederifolium

Eupatorium ligustrinum

Escallonia 'Iveyi' x5

Vinca difformis

Pot

Urn

Lawn

Hedera colchica 'Sulphur Heart'

Catalpa bignonioides

Pot

Solomon's Seal Polygonatum x hybridum x15

Scilla siberica

Helleborus orientalis x12

Aralia elata 'Aureovariegata' with Sarcococca humilis

Hedera colchica 'Sulphur Heart'

Parthenocissus tricuspidata Veitchii

Lonicera x purpusii

Path

Astrantia major 'Sunningdale Variegated' x9

Hosta 'Royal Standard' x7

Shed

Choisya ternata x5

Nicotiana sylvestris x9

Rosa 'Frühlingsgold'

Hebe rakaiensis

Cistus 'Silver Pink'

Parthenocissus tricuspidata 'Veitchii'

Verbascum 'Vernale' x3

Celastrus orbiculatus

Solanum crispum 'Glasnevin'

Clematis 'Bill Mackenzie'

Artemisia arborescens 'Faith Raven'

shrubs have had to go or be severely trimmed back, but in essence it is still the garden I designed in 1986, and brings back memories of my part in the original concept.

Once the overall design was agreed on, it only remained to fill in the details and complete the planting plans. The garden – only 30m (100ft) long and 7m (22ft) wide, and running south from the house – is planned for seasonal progression, with some climber or shrub flowering almost every month. These, bulked up along the perimeter walls, make a frame for the garden, turning it into a secret oasis. The London microclimate allows for lots of experimental planting, especially with decorative evergreen shrubs and climbers. Roses, perennials and annuals – tulips alternating with tobacco plants – give colour in the flowerbeds from spring to autumn.

The rose 'New Dawn', tied to the trellis-work, has two prolific flowering seasons. Nearby, arching *Ceanothus* 'Cascade' makes a blue mist in spring near the house, and its evergreen foliage provides a neighbourly screen all year. Another evergreen, Winter's bark (*Drimys winteri*) from the Magellan Straits, grows as a substantial pyramid, benefiting from wall protection and the favourable microclimate. Its May flowers are ivory-white and scented. Beyond the drimys and succeeding it in flowering sequence is the beauty bush (*Kolkwitzia amabilis* 'Pink Cloud'), elegant with flower in early June. The horizontally branched American dogwood *Cornus alternifolia* 'Argentea', with its silver variegated leaves, green edged with cream, forms an architectural feature. A blue potato flower (*Solanum crispum* 'Glasnevin')

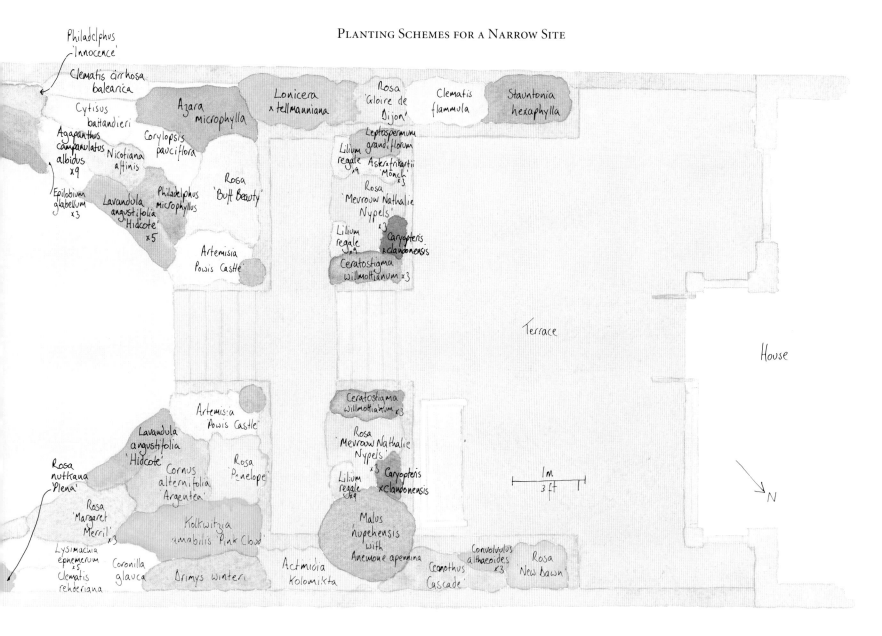

Philadelphus 'Innocence'

Clematis cirrhosa balearica

Cytisus battandieri

Azara microphylla

Lonicera x tellmanniana

Rosa 'Gloire de Dijon'

Clematis flammula

Stauntonia hexaphylla

Agapanthus campanulatus albidus x9

Corylopsis pauciflora

Nicotiana affinis

Leptospermum grandiflorum

Lilium regale x9

Aster x frikartii 'Mönch'

Rosa 'Mevrouw Nathalie Nypels'

Epilobium glabellum x3

Philadelphus microphyllus

Lavandula angustifolia 'Hidcote' x5

Rosa 'Buff Beauty'

Lilium regale

Caryopteris x clandonensis

x3

Artemisia Powis Castle

Ceratostigma willmottianum x3

Terrace

House

Artemisia Powis Castle

Ceratostigma willmottianum x3

Lavandula angustifolia 'Hidcote'

Cornus alternifolia 'Argentea'

Rosa 'Penelope'

Rosa 'Mevrouw Nathalie Nypels'

Rosa nutkana 'Plena'

Lilium regale x9

Caryopteris x clandonensis

x3

Rosa 'Margaret Merril' x3

Kolkwitzia amabilis 'Pink Cloud'

Malus hupehensis with Anemone apennina

1m
3ft

N

Lysimachia ephemerum x5

Coronilla glauca

Drimys winteri

Actinidia Kolomikta

Ceanothus 'Cascade'

Convolvulus althaeoides x3

Rosa 'New Dawn'

Clematis rehderiana

flowers for many months; towering above lush plantings of glossy-leaved choisya, it also screens houses at the end of the garden. The late-flowering lemon-peel clematis (*C.* 'Bill MacKenzie') twines through other plants on the trellis.

On the opposite, east-facing side of the garden there is sun in the morning but afternoons are shady, with overhanging trees from the neighbour's garden. I put a tender scented climber near the house: *Stauntonia hexaphylla*, with large leathery green leaves and white racemes tinged with violet.

Further along, the evergreen *Azara microphylla* has vanilla-scented yellow puff flowers, stamens rather than petals, in early spring, while nearby the Moroccan broom (*Cytisus battandieri*), with laburnum-like grey leaves, has pineapple-scented cone-shaped yellow flower clusters in June. Honeysuckles and clematis, including the shade-tolerant honeysuckle *Lonicera* x *tellmanniana*, also clamber on this east-facing wall. At the far end, by the path, there is a group of camellias – unfortunately they are in quite the wrong position, as early

morning sun can damage flowerbuds after frost.

As the borders broaden out at the further end to encircle the lawn, the planting is more sombre: mainly green leaves and white flowers, although there are touches of colour. Carpets of blue scilla grow below around hellebores and astrantia. Under the spreading branches of the catalpa, the mass of winter-flowering periwinkle (*Vinca difformis*) is kept tidily back to allow autumn-flowering cyclamen (*C. hederifolium*) to flourish in their season.

A FLOWER-CLAD PERGOLA IN A COUNTRY GARDEN

ABOVE *The main vista from the drawing-room leads to a venerable apple tree, past hedges of white rugosa roses, and on to the woods in the distance. To the left, the beauty bush (Kolkwitzia amabilis) can be seen in full flower at the end of the pergola.*

RIGHT *The view along the pergola to the house, in midsummer almost hidden by blossom and cascading roses, with the beauty bush on the left.*

The garden belonging to Mr and Mrs Peter Land was one of the first I worked on and, when I went back there in 1996, it was almost nine years since I had last visited it. Gillian Lynne is a choreographer and Peter Land a dancer, and their life as artists is reflected in the restoration of the buildings and garden: an old stable block, for example, has been skilfully converted into an exercise room and indoor swimming pool. I was very excited to renew acquaintance with the garden and see dense yew hedges, planted in 1987, creating architectural barriers; roses and honeysuckle cascading over the pergola; and plants in the house border brimming over their allotted spaces. All in all, a general feeling of maturity.

I was invited to participate in the

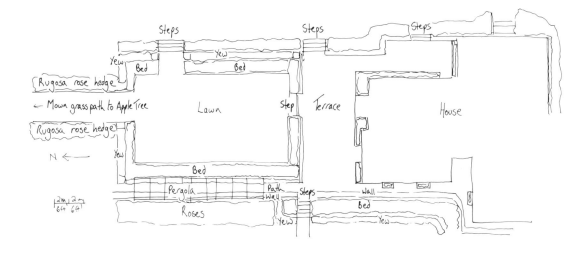

22

restoration of this Gloucestershire garden soon after I started designing seriously. I believe I was offered the job on the strength of my book, *Colour in Your Garden*, which had been published in 1985 and which the clients had seen. That book, still in print today, was a 'watershed' for me, and marked the real beginning of a writing and designing career. How fortunate I have been.

The seventeenth-century house with a medieval core, almost encircled by a hanging wood under the Cotswold escarpment, has wonderful views down the valley into the countryside. Much loved, and planted with many interesting trees by previous owners, the garden did not need radical redesigning but was overgrown and in need of a facelift. As so often happens, trees and shrubs had encroached on flowerbeds, necessitating thinning and rationalization, and new areas for flowers.

The house lies almost at the bottom of a slope. Steep banks and some retaining walls shelter the back of it against the hill; terraces and level spaces surround it. I was primarily concerned with flowerbeds and terraces to the south of the house. On an upper level I designed a broad pergola to extend the architecture of the house, a flowerbed 'bank' below it. At the south end of the main lawn, hedges of white rugosa roses were aligned on an ancient apple tree, to be glimpsed through a gap in a new double alley of yew.

RIGHT *On higher ground behind the pergola, hybrid musk roses, which flower brilliantly twice each season, are surrounded by peonies: old-fashioned* Paeonia officinalis *to tumble over the wall, and – in front beside the roses and slightly later in flowering – cultivars of P. lactiflora, including 'White Wings', 'Bowl of Beauty' and scented 'Duchesse de Nemours'. Bushes of blue-flowered* Caryopteris x clandonensis *take over at the end of the summer.*

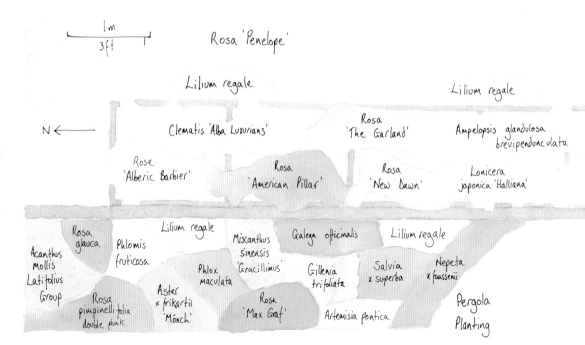

Rosa 'Buff Beauty'

Rosa Felicia

Rosa 'Celeste'

Pink Peonies

Lilium regale

Lilium regale

Clematis rehderiana

Rosa 'White Cockade'

Rosa 'Bobbie James'

Rosa 'Gloire de Dijon'

Lonicera japonica 'Halliana'

Rosa 'Félicité Perpétue'

Rosa 'American Pillar'

Rosa 'Cécile Brünner'

Lilium regale

Galega orientalis

Miscanthus sinensis 'Gracillimus'

Lilium regale

Phlomis anatolica

Phlox maculata 'Omega'

Lilium regale

Eupatorium purpureum 'Atropurpureum'

Nepeta x faassenii

Salvia x superba

Kniphofia 'Maid of Orleans'

Aster amellus 'King George'

Coreopsis verticillata 'Moonbeam'

Aruncus dioicus 'Kneiffii'

Astrantia major

Rosa pimpinellifolia double white

Artemisia pontica

Rosa 'Raubritter'

The first thing to be done was the construction of the pergola along an existing path running out at right angles to the house and main south-facing terrace. Reached by steep steps rising up the hill at the side of the house, which also lead to the wilder garden above, the pergola provided space for a planted bank and lawn as an extension of the terrace below.

The old terrace shapes and steps were retained where possible – as were old herringbone cotoneasters which gave character to the site – but there was much new planting. To give a less flat effect, we edged the terrace with lavender, and widened the house beds so that both the house and the terraces wrapped around it could be thickly planted. Today, luxuriant choisyas frame the front-door steps, and myrtles, corokia, Jerusalem sage, ceanothus, *Abelia x grandiflora* and a flourishing evergreen 'laburnum', *Piptanthus nepalensis* (among my favourite plants for a sheltered site) confirm my original design. The main borders on the slope under the pergola, partly edged with catmint, are planted with a sweep of broad-leaved acanthus near the terraces, shrub roses, red hot pokers, lilies, astrantias and late-flowering blue asters (*Aster amellus* 'King George' and *A.* x *frikartii* 'Mönch'). Above and behind the pergola, peonies for spring, hybrid musk roses for early summer, and blue-flowered caryopteris for later, establish a theme.

LEFT *An inviting view along the path from the shady end of the pergola above the house. Over the years, lady's mantle* (Alchemilla mollis) *has self-seeded in the gravel, but the clipped line of box, together with walls and steps, holds the structure of the design together.*

A City Garden in Compartments

ABOVE *By an elegant seat at the end of the garden, euphorbia (E. characias ssp.* wulfenii*), foxgloves and annual white cosmos grow in cottage-style profusion. The vertical accents of the foxglove and the spiky leaves of the New Zealand flax contrast with more rounded shapes to give the garden coherence. Self-seeders plug gaps in flowerbeds and also give a romantic and informal air to a garden.*

Nicholas and Susannah Horton-Fawkes moved to Islington in north London in 1986. I had already been advising them about the garden at their main home in Yorkshire and they asked me to help them with their new garden. The narrow space, 14m (45ft) long and 4m (14ft) wide, and orientated east to west, is typical of a town garden. At the eastern end, immediately behind the house, a large old black-barked pear tree creates a wide circle of shade, and neighbouring trees to the north also create shade along the perimeter border. In fact, the garden is so narrow that even perimeter planting on the south or west sides, while increasing privacy, simply increases the shade.

Both Nicholas and Susannah were already knowledgeable gardeners and we all agreed about what was appropriate for the design layout: the garden was to be divided into compartments by hedges and strong-boned shrubs. Each section was to have a slightly different planting emphasis. A path was needed along the north-facing bed to link the different 'rooms' and provide an axis with a view up and down the garden on its south side. The planting was to be simple but thick enough along the perimeters to provide privacy. On paper this was a classical use of space, and as a design it has worked well.

I used brick paving for the path, for areas between beds, and for a larger sitting area at the far end of the garden. The planting proved to be a problem as the garden matured. My plan used simple plants and concentrated on scent and form rather than riots of bright colour: acid-yellow euphorbias for spring; blue catmint, white philadelphus and creamy roses to reach a peak in June; mauve lavenders and blue agapanthus for later in the summer. Early-flowering shrubs were to include an informal hedge of the very fragrant *Viburnum carlesii*, grown as standards and underplanted with 'Margaret Merril' roses, but the viburnums were unobtainable that year so Portugal laurels were used as a replacement, and the garden soon became too shady for the roses.

In sun, just beyond the pear tree, a square bed edged with dwarf box (*Buxus sempervirens* 'Suffruticosa') framed black tulips, black violas and the inky-leaved form of lilyturf (*Ophiopogon planiscapus* 'Nigrescens') with tall white tobacco plants (*Nicotiana sylvestris*) to round off the summer. This area has become increasingly shaded and ferns and hostas now grow there in gravel. A hedge of taller box (*B. sempervirens* 'Handsworthiensis') frames hellebores, *Smyrnium perfoliatum*, and sarcococcas for winter scent, underneath the pear tree. The north-facing border was for foliage plants such as erythroniums, hostas, Solomon's seal, toadlilies (*Tricyrtis formosana* Stolonifera Group) and late-flowering wood

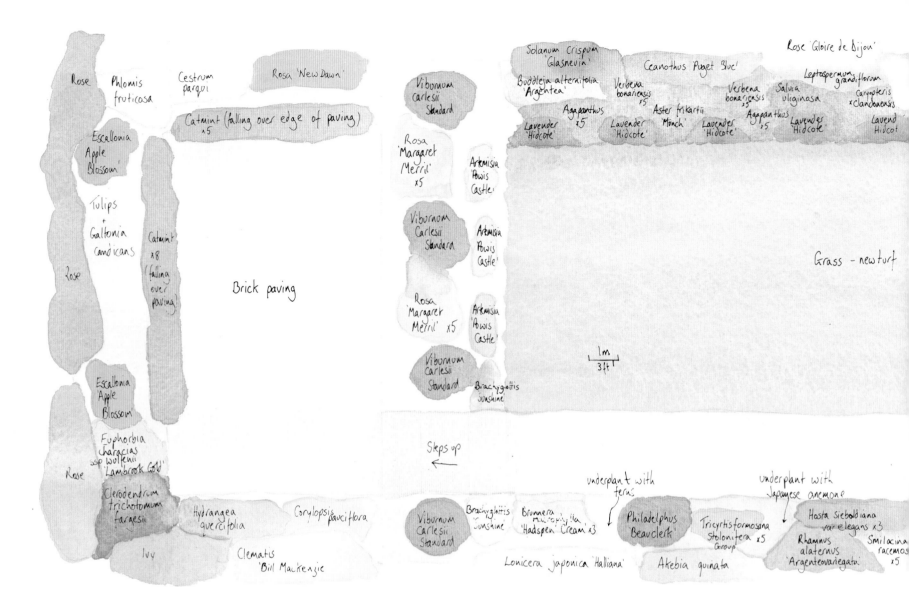

Rose
Phlomis fruticosa
Cestrum parqui
Rosa 'New Dawn'
Catmint (falling over edge of paving) x5
Escallonia 'Apple Blossom'
Tulips + Galtonia candicans
Rose
Catmint x8 (falling over paving)
Brick paving
Escallonia 'Apple Blossom'
Euphorbia characias ssp wulfenii 'Lambrook Gold'
Rose
Clerodendrum trichotomum fargesii
Ivy
Hydrangea quercifolia
Clematis 'Bill Mackenzie'
Corylopsis pauciflora

Viburnum carlesii Standard
Rosa 'Margaret Merril' x5
Artemisia 'Powis Castle'
Viburnum Carlesii Standard
Artemisia 'Powis Castle'
Rosa 'Margaret Merril' x5
Artemisia 'Powis Castle'
Viburnum Carlesii Standard
Brachyglottis Sunshine

Solanum Crispum 'Glasnevin'
Rose 'Gloire de Dijon'
Buddleja alternifolia 'Argentea'
Ceanothus 'Puget Blue'
Verbena bonariensis x5
Verbena bonariensis x5
Salvia uliginosa
Leptospermum grandiflorum
Caryopteris x Clandonensis
Agapanthus x5
Aster frikartii 'Mönch'
Agapanthus x5
Lavender 'Hidcote'
Lavender 'Hidcote'
Lavender 'Hidcote'
Lavender 'Hidcote'
Lavender 'Hidcote'
Lavend 'Hidcot'

Grass – new turf

1m / 3ft

Steps up ←

Viburnum Carlesii Standard
Brachyglottis Sunshine
Brunnera macrophylla 'Hadspen Cream' x3
underplant with ferns
Philadelphus 'Beauclerk'
underplant with Japanese anemone
Hosta Sieboldiana var elegans x3
Tricyrtis formosana stolonifera Group x5
Rhamnus alaternus 'Argenteovariegata'
Smilacina racemosa x5
Lonicera japonica 'Halliana'
Akebia quinata

asters (*Aster divaricatus*) canopied by June-flowering philadelphus and a tall 'John Downie' crab apple.

In spite of the shade, the Horton-Fawkeses also wanted a lawn – a central green 'well' which would become a focal point of light as well as a comfortable sitting area. The lawn was installed, but after a year proved so poor that it had to be abandoned, and was replaced with brick paving to match the other areas.

While much of the design was really a collaboration between me and Susannah, the original planting suggestions were mine.

They were based on the flowers that I knew Susannah liked, and this sheltered London garden gave us an opportunity to use some favourite plants which would not have proved hardy in the Horton-Fawkeses' cold exposed garden in Yorkshire. What we did not allow for was the fact that the London garden would need a lot of maintenance. The plans I made included many plants that are normally strong and healthy in open environments; in the enclosed London atmosphere they proved to need constant – almost daily – attention. Some help was available with general maintenance, but

routine spraying for white fly on roses, for black fly on philadelphus and silver-leaved plants, and for mildew was just not possible. As a result, over the years Susannah has replaced many of the choicer disease- and pest-prone plants with hostas and ferns, which are more tolerant of the environment.

Thus, although the main 'bones' of the garden remain unaltered, the plants have been considerably changed. The garden is now a green oasis with incidents of mainly white flowers – at their best in the evening light. Hidden, private and discreet, it is serenely beautiful.

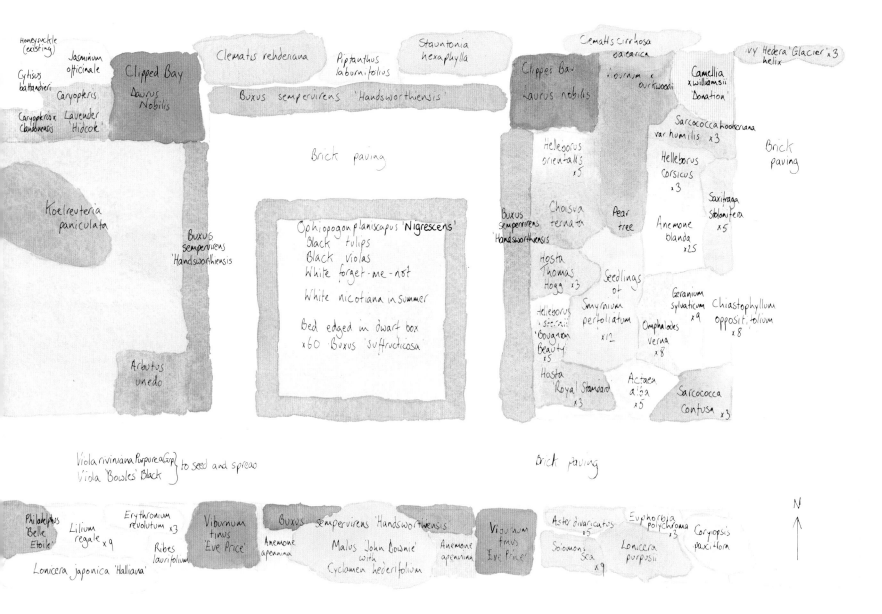

Honeysuckle (existing)

Jasminum officinale

Cytisus battandieri

Caryopteris

Caryopteris x Clandonensis

Lavender 'Hidcote'

Clipped Bay
Laurus Nobilis

Clematis rehderiana

Piptanthus laburnifolius

Stauntonia hexaphylla

Clematis cirrhosa balearica

Clipped Bay
Laurus nobilis

Viburnum x burkwoodii

Ivy Hedera 'Glacier' x 3 helix

Camellia x williamsii 'Donation'

Buxus sempervirens 'Handsworthiensis'

Brick paving

Koelreuteria paniculata

Buxus sempervirens 'Handsworthiensis'

Sarcococca hookeriana var humilis x 3

Brick paving

Helleborus orientalis x 5

Helleborus corsicus x 3

Saxifraga stolonifera x 5

Buxus sempervirens 'Handsworthiensis'

Choisya ternata

Pear tree

Anemone blanda x 25

Ophiopogon planiscapus 'Nigrescens'
Black tulips
Black violas
White forget-me-not

White nicotiana in summer

Bed edged in dwarf box
x 60 Buxus 'suffruticosa'

Hosta Thomas Hogg x 3

Seedlings of Smyrnium perfoliatum x 12

Geranium sylvaticum x 9

Chiastophyllum oppositifolium x 8

Helleborus sternii 'Boughton Beauty' x 5

Omphalodes verna x 8

Arbutus unedo

Hosta 'Royal Standard' x 3

Actaea alba x 5

Sarcococca confusa x 3

Brick paving

Viola riviniana Purpurea Group
Viola 'Bowles' Black
} to seed and spread

Philadelphus 'Belle Etoile'

Lilium regale x 9

Erythronium revolutum x 3

Ribes laurifolium

Viburnum tinus 'Eve Price'

Anemone apennina

Buxus sempervirens 'Handsworthiensis'

Malus 'John Downie' with Cyclamen hederifolium

Anemone apennina

Viburnum tinus 'Eve Price'

Aster divaricatus x 5

Solomon's Seal x 9

Euphorbia polychroma x 3

Lonicera purpusii

Corylopsis paucifolia

Lonicera japonica 'Halliana'

N ↑

LEFT *A cranesbill geranium (G. x magnificum) and a self-seeded foxglove straggle through the mesh of one of the elegant seats in the end garden room.*

RIGHT *The climbing rose 'New Dawn' almost envelopes another of the metal seats in the end garden room. Seats, even if seldom used for resting, can be placed to end vistas and 'anchor' the eye in a garden.*

Looking from the middle compartment to the end of the garden, where brachyglottis, cosmos and Japanese anemones are planted in profusion around the standard laurels. The warm still air in this small London plot brings numerous pests and diseases and the garden needs constant attention *and 'manicuring': dead leaves have to be swept up and dying flowerheads and foliage pruned away. Most of the shrubs need cutting back each year, sometimes more than once – the evergreens in spring and deciduous shrubs in the winter.*

Looking back towards the house. Portugal laurels frame the middle compartment of the garden. This area is now paved with brick, as grass failed to thrive in the shade. Near the house the lush planting – probably too tightly packed in the original 1986 plan – has flowed over the edges of the beds. Ferns and other shade-tolerant perennials have replaced much of the original planting. In this predominantly 'green' garden, the white flowers glow restfully in evening light.

A Shady Town Garden

In 1987 I was asked to help with the design of a garden in the rue de Bellechasse in Paris. Close to the left bank of the Seine and a stone's throw from Les Invalides and the Musée d'Orsay, by Parisian standards the garden is a large one: 33m x 23m (110ft x 80ft), so this was an exciting opportunity. But when I first visited it, I could see only the problems – the mature horse chestnuts and other trees creating deep shade in summer and taking much of the moisture from the soil in the western 15m (50ft) of the garden, the dull walls dominating the views from the main terrace leading into the garden (still to be laid at that time), and poor soil throughout.

The shade we have learnt to live with, just, because the trees do give an appropriate sense of balance to the house and screen a rather uninteresting building (in any event the city would never allow them to be felled, although they do permit judicious pruning and thinning). The blank wall has been decorated with sophisticated stucco and wisterias trained as pillars between the windows will eventually widen out and join to make the walls of the neighbouring apartment an attractive feature. The slightly alkaline soil is continually being improved and enriched.

In fact, my only regret concerns the soil. We discussed bringing in new topsoil at the beginning, but at the time I felt the expense was not justified. This is a mistake I would never make today. As a general principle, I would far rather spend available funds on soil and its preparation even though, for more modest clients, it may lead to temporary economies in garden features or

ABOVE *The view across the garden from the terrace to the neighbouring apartment. Wisteria is beginning to spread across the wall.*

RIGHT *Looking along the pear walk from the end of the terrace to a statue backed by an evergreen magnolia. These beds, originally planted with the rose 'Mevrouw Nathalie Nypels' and catmint, have since been simplified and have mainly white flowers such as* Galtonia candicans.

plants. In the case of the rue de Bellechasse it was a foolish and quite unnecessary economy, and the soil will never be quite as it should be.

The garden is almost square, and from the start we agreed that we needed a central lawn – a well of light and soothing green in the middle of the city. This meant that other features would be arranged around the grass. We decided to make a Woodland Garden at the shady end where grass would not thrive, while gravel paths, lined with granite setts and low clipped hedges of box (*Buxus sempervirens* 'Handsworthiensis') would make a route around the garden and cross it in front of the 'wood'. In the north-west corner of the garden, on a diagonal with the main terrace, a small garden house – once a garage – would become a guest house (it is now the owner's office). This needed its own separate yet connected garden space. Now in front of it are two small box and gravel Parterre Gardens, planted with autumn-flowering cyclamen (*Cyclamen hederifolium*) with clipped hemispheres at the corners (copied from the Villa Caponi in Italy).

By the main terrace, built with old limestone flags, Portugal laurel (*Prunus lusitanica*) clipped individually into rounded shapes, gives a sense of privacy as well as evergreen interest in winter, and wisterias and tender climbers with scented flowers, such as *Trachelospermum jasminoides*, grow on the house walls. From the end of the terrace an axial path, lined with callery pears

LEFT ABOVE *The lawn and shady guest house corner with its parterres of box and gravel.*

LEFT *Clipped trees and hedges play an important role in defining the design of this garden. Lawn and box, pears and Portugal laurel are all different shades of green that change with the seasons and after clipping.*

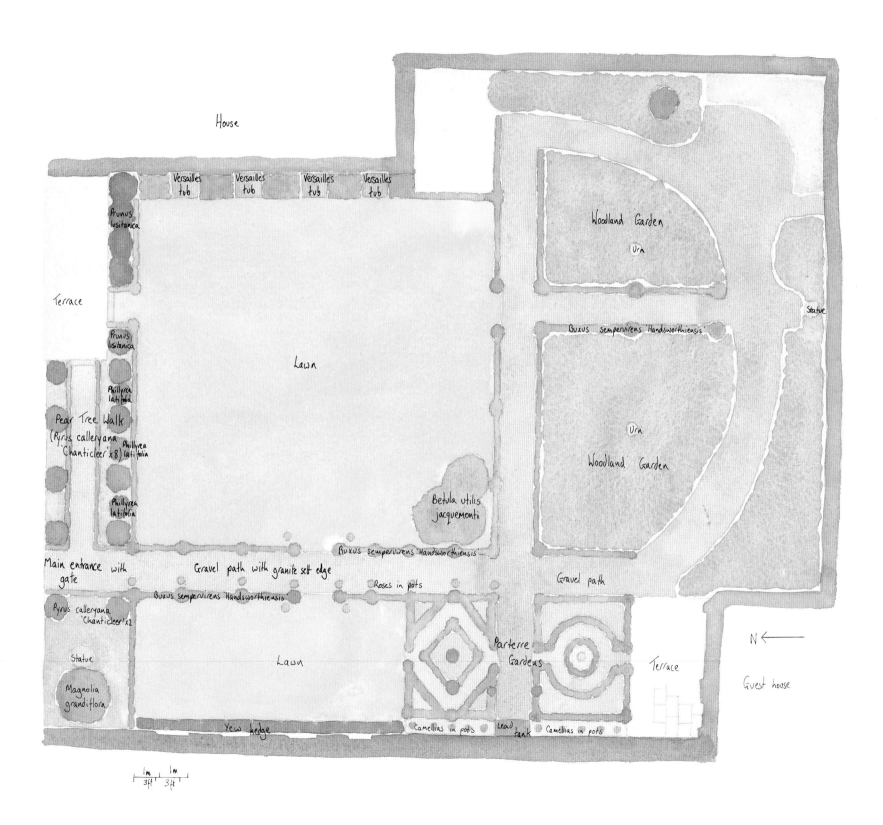

House

Versailles tub

Versailles tub

Versailles tub

Versailles tub

Prunus lusitanica

Terrace

Prunus lusitanica

Phillyrea latifolia

Pear Tree Walk
(*Pyrus calleryana* 'Chanticleer' x 8)

Phillyrea latifolia

Phillyrea latifolia

Lawn

Woodland Garden

Urn

Buxus sempervirens 'Handsworthiensis'

Statue

Betula utilis jacquemontii

Urn

Woodland Garden

Buxus sempervirens 'Handsworthiensis'

Main entrance with gate

Gravel path with granite sett edge

Buxus sempervirens 'Handsworthiensis'

Roses in pots

Gravel path

Pyrus calleryana 'Chanticleer' x2

Statue

Lawn

Parterre Gardens

Terrace

Magnolia grandiflora

N ←

Guest house

Yew hedge

Camellias in pots

Lead tank

Camellias in pots

1m 1m
3ft 3ft

(*Pyrus calleryana* 'Chanticleer') in box-edged beds, leads to a statue backed by an evergreen magnolia (*Magnolia grandiflora*). Under the house windows, large custom-made Versailles planters are filled with white tulips in spring and white pelargoniums throughout the summer. Between them are tightly manicured 'cubes' of box.

To divide the lawn area from the Woodland Garden, I put in a loosely grown hedge of *Choisya ternata* around the base of the trees. A central path, today edged with oak-leaved hydrangeas and white-flowered *Rubus* 'Benenden', leads through the wood to a statue flanked by shrubs under-planted with hostas, and on to a lattice-work sitting arbour which conceals a garden shed.

Hydrangea anomala petiolaris and ivies succeed on the shady walls, while scented winter-flowering sarcococcas frame corners by the guest house with *Daphne odora* 'Aureomarginata' and the yellow *Daphne pontica*; but getting plants to flower in the dense woodland shade is difficult. Winter-flowering laurustinus (forms of *Viburnum tinus*) are, like the fragrant *Lonicera* x *purpusii*, reliable flowering standbys and we have experimented with most of the available shade-tolerant shrubs and perennials. We have planted a great number of shrubs with

LEFT, ABOVE *The arbour in the wood is a hybrid between a Victorian conceit at Tatton Park in Cheshire and the arbours on the corners of beds at Villandry in France. Painted blue-grey, the arbour picks up the colour of the glaucous-leaved hostas. White lilies and hosta flowers scent this secluded sitting area.*

LEFT *With adequate moisture, the oak-leaf hydrangea* (Hydrangea quercifolia)*, flowers well in the deep shade of the Woodland Garden.*

glossy leaves whose shining surfaces make up for lack of flowers. The foliage of sarcococcas, Alexandrian laurel (*Danae racemosa*), various osmanthus (recently added) and above all of choisyas, glow throughout the year. We have also used golden-leaved shrubs to give colour: golden privets, golden euonymus (*E. japonicus*), golden-leaved philadelphus (*P. coronarius* 'Aureus'), and *Physocarpus opulifolius* 'Luteus'. Two silver-variegated buckthorns (*Rhamnus alaternus* 'Argenteovariegata') today make splashes of light by the guest house and the arbour.

Under the shrubs we have planted shade-tolerant perennials and cyclamen. White-flowered Japanese anemones (*Anemone* x *hybrida* 'Honorine Jobert'), European gingers (*Asarum europaeum*) with glossy leaves, *Alchemilla mollis*, ferns (including the Japanese painted fern, *Athyrium niponicum* var. *pictum*), more recently the bright blue *Corydalis flexuosa*, hellebores (forms of *Helleborus orientalis*), hostas (some with variegated leaves) and foamflower (*Tiarella cordifolia*) are all beginning to succeed.

I have found the climate in Paris milder than I expected, due to the heat generated by buildings and people. There is also an automatic watering system, though it has not always worked efficiently. However, while we can ensure that the shrubs, well watered and fertilized, are vigorous and healthy, we cannot always coax them into flower in the darkest corners. A large rambling rose on the arbour is still searching to reach the light and flower.

This garden, so fraught with difficulty at the outset, is a success, although the owner would prefer more flowers and colour and we are now discussing the possibility of making a flower-filled parterre under the neighbours' wall. Like all good gardens, this one will never stand still.

ABOVE Hydrangea aspera *ssp.* sargentiana

ABOVE Viburnum plicatum *'Mariesii'*
BELOW Helleborus orientalis

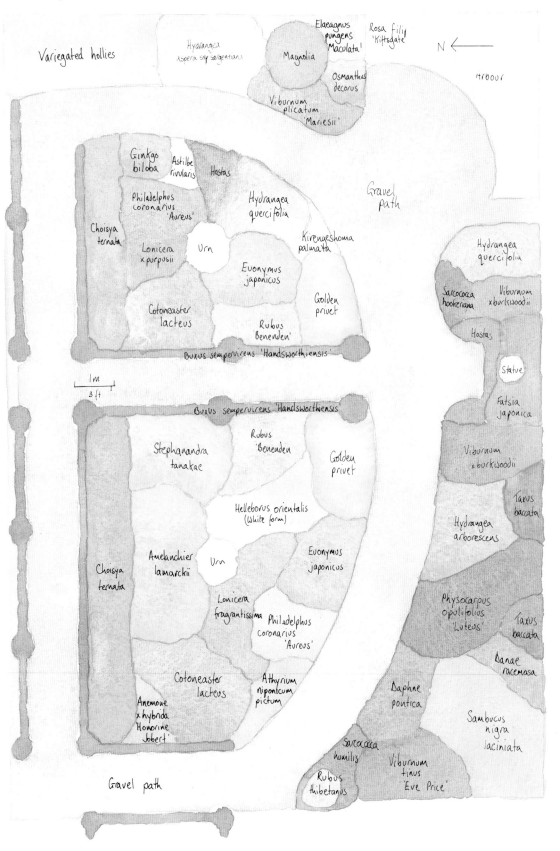

Variegated hollies

Hydrangea aspera ssp sargentiana

Elaeagnus pungens 'Maculata'

Rosa filip 'Kiftsgate'

N

Magnolia

Osmanthus decorus

Arbour

Viburnum plicatum 'Mariesii'

Ginkgo biloba

Astilbe rivularis

Hastas

Hydrangea quercifolia

Gravel path

Philadelphus coronarius 'Aureus'

Choisya ternata

Urn

Kirengeshoma palmata

Hydrangea quercifolia

Lonicera x purpusii

Euonymus japonicus

Sarcococca hookeriana

Viburnum x burkwoodii

Cotoneaster lacteus

Golden privet

Rubus 'Benenden'

Hastas

Buxus sempervirens 'Handsworthiensis'

Statue

1 m
3 ft

Buxus sempervirens 'Handsworthiensis'

Fatsia japonica

Stephanandra tanakae

Rubus 'Benenden'

Golden privet

Viburnum x burkwoodii

Helleborus orientalis (White form)

Hydrangea arborescens

Taxus baccata

Choisya ternata

Amelanchier lamarckii

Urn

Euonymus japonicus

Lonicera fragrantissima

Philadelphus coronarius 'Aureus'

Physocarpus opulifolius 'Luteus'

Taxus baccata

Cotoneaster lacteus

Athyrium niponicum pictum

Danae racemosa

Anemone x hybrida 'Honorine Jobert'

Daphne pontica

Sambucus nigra laciniata

Sarcococca humilis

Viburnum tinus 'Eve Price'

Rubus thibetanus

Gravel path

A WINDSWEPT ISLAND GARDEN

The Inner Hebridean island of Oronsay, off the west coast of Scotland, has a rich history. It is said that in the sixth century Saint Columba, travelling in a rowing boat from Ireland to teach Christianity to the heathen Scots, first landed on this small island before continuing on his way to establish a community on Iona. In the fourteenth century an extensive Augustinian Priory was founded, in which the monks would have grown medicinal and useful herbs, and vegetables.

The Augustinian Priory is now a distinguished ruin but the site is a romantic and ancient one. Today, of the considerable fourteenth-century complex, only the Prior's house remains roofed, the church and cloisters as well as the priory itself lie open to the sky. In the churchyard, the fine Oronsay Cross, carved in about 1500, still stands.

The island of Oronsay is small – about 10 sq kilometres (less than 4 sq miles) in all, and is connected at low tide by a strand to the larger island of Colonsay. From Ben Oronsay, the highest point of the island, there are breathtaking views across the water to Jura and Islay, and corncrakes still thrive where grass lies uncut until after nesting. Salt winds batter the land for most of the year and there are no deep valleys where trees can grow protected from equinoctial and winter storms. Nevertheless, situated as the island is in the path of the Atlantic Gulf Stream Drift,

there are many horticultural compensations. Frosts seldom occur and rainfall is generally 113cm (45in) a year – far less heavy and oppressive than in the mountains of Jura just further east.

With my first husband and my children, I had been a regular summer tenant in Oronsay all through the 1970s, and going back to make a garden here was one of the most exciting and emotional projects I have undertaken. The garden was to be made for a well-known architect and his wife, from Boston, Massachusetts, who had bought the whole island. By 1989 they had sensitively stabilized the Priory ruins and restored the farm buildings and cottages. The original 2m (7ft) stone walls had been repaired and a farming partner had been installed. I was asked to transform what had recently been a winter feeding yard for cattle into an ornamental and kitchen garden, surrounded by ancient walls on a site that had almost certainly been the original herb and vegetable garden to the Augustinian Priory.

It was a challenge, too, to work for an architect with a trained 'eye'. Fortunately, we agreed from the beginning that the garden must be divided up into a series of 'rooms', with winds funnelled into short rather than long stretches – with the result that the final plan on paper, apart from extended cross alleys of grass, almost resembled a maze in its complexity.

ABOVE *The view through the garden to the north, from the Medieval Garden with its cobbled path. The privet hedges are growing strongly. The square central bed is planted with the apothecary rose (Rosa gallica var. officinalis), and other plants known in the fourteenth century complete the picture.*

The owners' American home on the other side of the Atlantic is a cliff-top house on the North Shore of Boston, so it seemed appropriate to introduce an American theme and one which reflected the shared ocean. I recalled the privet hedges used as windbreaks at the eastern end of Long Island, and privet hedges – now in their prime but originally protected by fencing – were planted to give permanent structure. These marked out the pattern of the longer alleys and inner divisions. In the smaller compartments

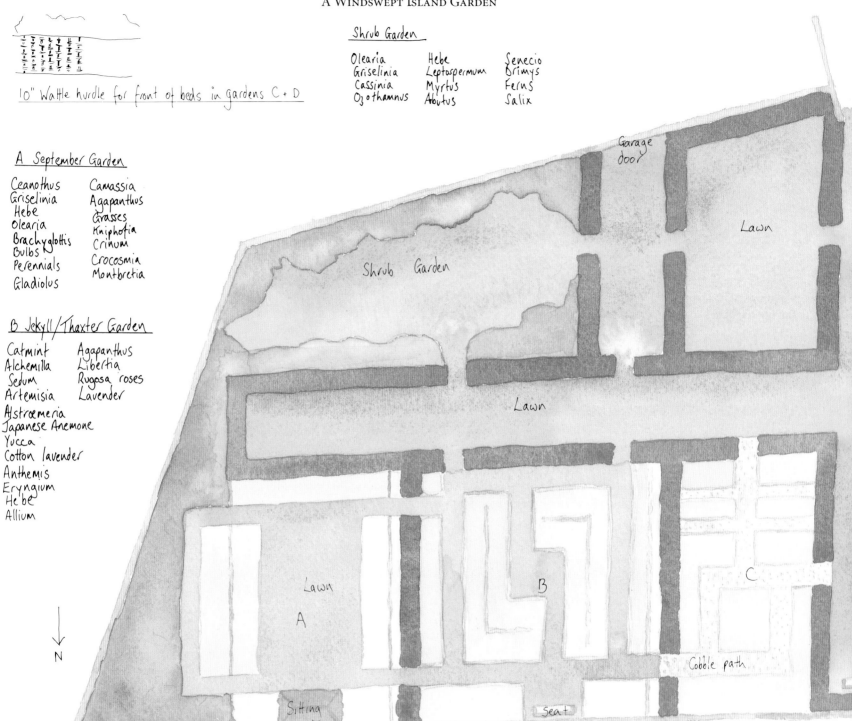

10" Wattle hurdle for front of beds in gardens C + D

Shrub Garden

Olearia	Hebe	Senecio
Griselinia	Leptospermum	Drimys
Cassinia	Myrtus	Ferns
Ozothamnus	Arbutus	Salix

A September Garden

Ceanothus	Camassia
Griselinia	Agapanthus
Hebe	Grasses
Olearia	Kniphofia
Brachyglottis	Crinum
Bulbs	Crocosmia
Perennials	Montbretia
Gladiolus	

B Jekyll/Thaxter Garden

Catmint	Agapanthus
Alchemilla	Libertia
Sedum	Rugosa roses
Artemisia	Lavender
Alstroemeria	
Japanese Anemone	
Yucca	
Cotton lavender	
Anthemis	
Eryngium	
Hebe	
Allium	

C Medieval Garden

Iris	Rue
Burnet rose	Alchemilla
Columbine	Anthemis
Silene	Wallflowers
Armeria	Rosemary

Poppies	Fennel
Violets	Dill
Soapwort	Chives

Cordon fruit on wall.

D Peony Garden

Paeonia mascula
Paeonia officinalis
Paeonia lactiflora
Lilium speciosum
Galtonia candicans
Cordon fruit on wall

E Early Summer Garden

Ceanothus	Camassia
Griselinia	Agapanthus
Hebe	Perennials
Olearia	
Brachyglottis	
Bulbs	

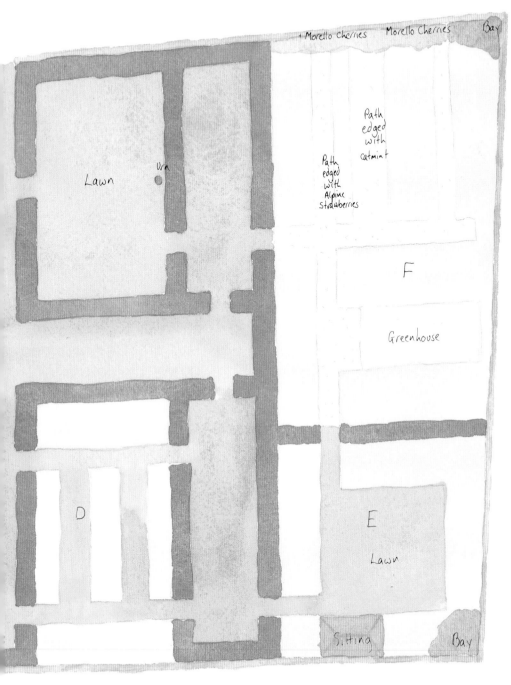

Morello cherries Morello Cherries Bay

Lawn

Urn

Path edged with catmint

Path edged with Alpine strawberries

F

Greenhouse

D

E

Lawn

Sitting

Bay

1m / 3ft 1m / 3ft

F. Vegetable Garden

Early potatoes
Tomatoes
Broad beans
Lettuces
Baby carrots
Swiss chard
Asparagus

Courgettes
Runner beans
Spinach

Raspberries
Japanese wineberries
Loganberries
Gooseberries

TOP Walls, cobbled paths and hurdles around the newly planted beds in the Medieval Garden, with Ben Oronsay behind.

ABOVE Geranium palmatum *from the Canaries is a prolific seeder. Conditions for this tender large-leaved monocarpic geranium are perfect. Rosemaries, French lavender, common yarrow* (Achillea millefolium), *germander* (Teucrium x lucidrys) *all grow luxuriantly inside the low willow hurdles.*

willow panels (especially woven in Somerset, but they could have been made by the monks in the fourteenth century from stunted willows on the island) gave extra wind protection. To add a further historical touch, I used low 25cm (10in) willow hurdles to contain many of the flowerbeds, so that each was 'raised' to make work easy – a medieval and monastic practice that I copied from early horticultural textbooks and engravings.

With the garden lying in full sun and exposed to the salt winds, there was no question of making a rhododendron garden or growing the many moisture-loving plants so typical of gardens in mainland Argyll. However, the open situation, air humidity and long summer days are perfect for most summer perennials, and exotics thrive beside tough old favourites. South African bulbs (agapanthus, kniphofias, galtonias) are planted below the walls and the flourishing hedges of Rugosa roses.

In each compartment I planned a garden with a different theme. The clients only intended to visit in May and September every year, so the garden to the west became an Early Summer Garden, and that to the east was planned for September. Today, except for spring bulbs and peonies, most of the early flowerers in the Early Summer

LEFT, ABOVE *Peruvian lilies (both* Alstroemeria ligtu *hybrids with pale pink flowers and the old* A. aurea *with vivid orange flowers) enjoy the conditions on Oronsay. Hebes – plants that are often too tender in inland counties of Great Britain – do well in this gentle climate and thrive in the salt-laden winds.*

LEFT, BELOW *The small catmint* Nepeta nervosa *grows comfortably inside the willow hurdles. If this plant succumbs in a hard winter, it is easily grown from seed and will flower in the first season. It will continue to flower all summer if regularly deadheaded.*

Garden have been abandoned in favour of a succession of flowers which have had a few months in which to recover from the winter gales: olearias, Rugosa roses, perovskias, lysimachias and asters. In the September Garden, tender hebes from New Zealand, able to withstand salt winds, also flourish with rugosa roses – some still in flower, some with scarlet hips.

In the centre, the enclosed Medieval Garden was planted – in a pattern outlined by cobbled paths – with plants which would have been familiar to the monks in the fourteenth century, many with curative or useful properties: the apothecary rose (*Rosa gallica* var. *officinalis*), woad (*Isatis tinctoria*), soapwort (*Saponaria officinalis*), rosemary, lavender, tansy, germander and artemisias with their fragrant leaves.

The idea for another garden came from Gertrude Jekyll and Celia Thaxter. Gertrude Jekyll made two island gardens, one at Lindisfarne Castle on Holy Island in Northumberland and another on Lambay Island in Dublin Bay, while Celia Thaxter, a contemporary of Miss Jekyll and the daughter of a lighthouse keeper in Maine, planted an annual garden at the turn of the century on Appledore, an island off the coast of southern Maine. Her beautiful garden, painted by the impressionist Childe Hassam, has recently been restored. The planting in my Jekyll/Thaxter garden has been chosen from their layouts: goat's rue, Jacob's ladder, hardy geraniums, verbenas, artemisias, sedums and catmints make a rich carpet.

In the Shrub Garden behind the barn there are more wind-tolerant New Zealanders – olearias, leptospermums, griselinias and hebes – which give shelter to lower-growing plants. A vegetable and fruit garden, with a small greenhouse, provides plenty of fresh produce. There are sitting places, protected from most winds, under the

south-facing walls. In this mild climate it is possible to enjoy the garden in every season.

In 1996 the Royal Society for the Protection of Birds were given a 10-year lease to manage the farming of the property, and the owners' estate manager and his wife, Donald and Eve Coleman, maintain and augment the garden. Many of the larger shrubs are regularly pruned back, and the original planting is continually adapted. The tender large-leaved *Geranium palmatum* from the Canaries knows no boundaries

and, like many other plants here, seeds happily in every part of the garden; a few non-medieval plants brighten the central Medieval Garden; and more permanent perennials and shrubs have replaced many of Celia Thaxter's annuals.

This is as it should be; a garden should never stand still. The important thing is that the garden retains its oasis-like quality – a cultivated paradise in a romantic wild landscape where, for much of the year, only buzzards and choughs soar overhead.

ABOVE *Looking east into the Peony Garden, most of the plantings are massed to give greatest effect. Lysimachias, eupatoriums and* Acidanthera 'Murieliae' *(now* Gladiolus callianthus 'Murieliae') *have taken the place of the peonies to give colour and interest later in the year than originally planned. The fencing, used initially to give protection to the privet hedges, has now been removed.*

ABOVE *Twining honeysuckles and small-flowered clematis – here* Lonicera x heckrottii *and* Clematis viticella *'Polish Spirit' – clothe the paired pillars of trelliswork on either side of the house.*

BELOW *A trellis archway, covered with Dutchman's pipe (a form of* Aristolochia*), allows a glimpse of the ornamental glasshouse.*

GARDENS WITHIN A GARDEN

There are two circumstances which helped to make the conception of this garden rather different from my normal experience. First, the plan I took with me on my flight to Detroit, made without ever having visited the site, was adopted almost without alteration. Secondly, I was lucky enough to be working with very visual and well-informed clients who already had a clear idea of the type of garden they wanted. This fortunately coincided exactly with my own ideas for the site.

I had a brief meeting with my clients in London a few weeks before my first visit and they provided me with a topographical plan and photographs. Their white-painted wooden house, also undergoing extensive alterations and restoration, was built at the end of the last century in a suburb of Detroit. It occupies a double block, measuring 30 x 35m/100 x 115 ft, on a suburban road. The house is set almost in the middle of the site and the main area of the garden is behind it, with an entrance driveway and room for beds on the roadside. My clients did not want a garden like most of those in the suburbs around the city of Detroit, which, with very cold winters (zone 5 for plants) and very hot summers, tend to consist of labour-saving trees and shrubs above groundcover of Baltic ivy, with summer colour provided by shade-tolerant busy lizzies in pink and white. Although not yet plantsmen, they were familiar with English-style Jekyll-inspired gardens and believed that with dedication it would be possible to create something similar in the extreme mid-western climate. They wanted a firm structure of hedges and evergreens to give definition during the cold winters, but with space for naturalistic cottage-like planting in flowerbeds for the summer months. They envisaged typical Gertrude Jekyll borders with weaving colours of roses, climbers, perennials and annuals.

This was my brief. Some structure had already been provided by a dark hedging of Canada hemlock (*Tsuga canadensis*) which lined and screened almost three sides of the garden, making a perfect background for later planting. I proposed that we should create a series of garden rooms, with front and back gardens connected by two parallel 'alleys'. Each corridor would provide privacy from the public roadway and also lead the eye along the walls of the house, and would terminate at the back perimeter in a small pavilion made of cedar laths. In front of the house the alleys are lined with free-standing pillars of trellis work, covered with honeysuckles and clematis. It was decided that behind the pavilions the hemlock hedging should be reinforced by a line of tall Bradford pears which, running along the back perimeter, would screen neighbouring houses. It would also give some immediate

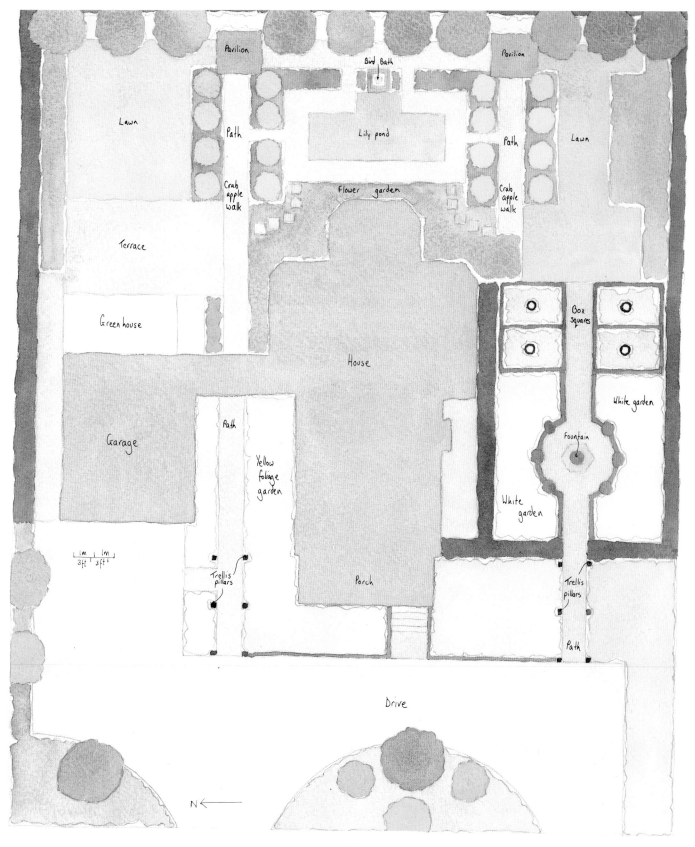

Pavilion

Bird Bath

Pavilion

Lawn

Path

Lily pond

Path

Lawn

Crab apple walk

Flower garden

Crab apple walk

Terrace

Box squares

Greenhouse

White garden

House

Garage

Fountain

Path

White garden

Yellow foliage garden

1m 1m
3ft 3ft

Trellis pillars

Porch

Trellis pillars

Path

Drive

N

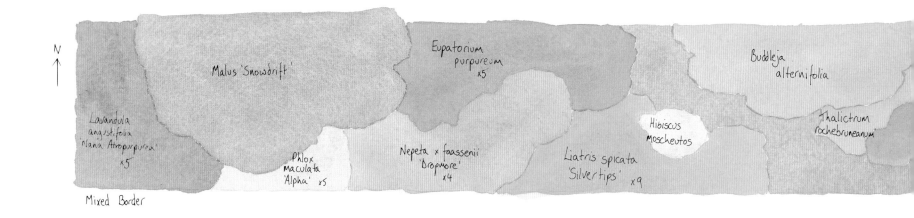

Malus 'Snowdrift'

Eupatorium
purpureum
x5

Buddleja
alternifolia

Lavandula
angustifolia
'Nana Atropurpurea'
x5

Hibiscus
Moscheutos

Thalictrum
rochebruneanum

Phlox
maculata
'Alpha' x5

Nepeta x faassenii
'Dropmore'
x4

Liatris spicata
'Silvertips' x9

Mixed Border

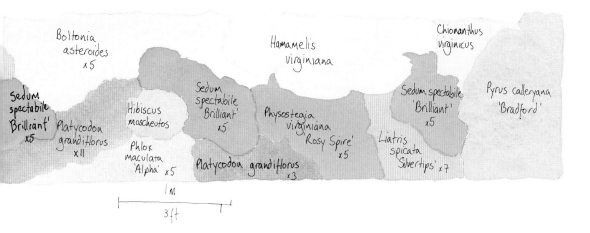

Sedum spectabile 'Brilliant' x5

Boltonia asteroides x5

Platycodon grandiflorus x11

Hibiscus moscheutos

Phlox maculata 'Alpha' x5

Sedum spectabile 'Brilliant' x5

Platycodon grandiflorus x3

Physostegia virginiana 'Rosy Spire' x5

Hamamelis virginiana

Liatris spicata 'Silvertips' x7

Sedum spectabile 'Brilliant' x5

Chionanthus virginicus

Pyrus calleryana 'Bradford'

1 M
3 ft

height to balance with the house.

Beyond the garage on the north side a sunny terrace looked out on to a lawn. Later an old ornamental glasshouse from Belgium was fitted in behind the garage and became one of the garden's most important features, providing a home for many tender plants during the cold winters. On one side of the lawn, I designed the Main Mixed Border to 'peak' towards the end of July, with comparatively drought- and heat-tolerant perennials such as thalictrums, eupatoriums, echinaceas, platycodons, liatris and physostegia. The shrubs – a mixture of deciduous and evergreen bushes – make a backbone down the centre of the bed to give some winter structure and interest, even when the garden is snow-covered – normally for a few months each year.

On the other side of the terrace, alleys of crab apple (*Malus* 'Snowdrift') add height and divide the garden into rooms. After flowering in spring – when their mass of white blossom contrasts with sheets of bugle (*Ajuga reptans*) at their feet – the heads of the crabs are pruned into compact shapes.

Directly behind the house, between the crab apple alleys, I added a formal pool edged with flowerbeds for roses, caryopteris,

artemisias and lavenders. Not all the 'permanent' plants in these beds are hardy through zone 5 winters, but shrubs with wood ripened by the heat are suprisingly resilient. As an insurance, cuttings are taken every year. Throughout the pool area, seedlings (appropriately referred to as 'volunteers' in America) such as centranthus, *Verbena bonariensis* and violas, are encouraged to find places in the cracks between the paving slates.

On the other side of the house, there was to be a formal box garden, centred on a fountain, mainly planted with white flowers. Shrubs give bulk and winter definition with drifts of summer-flowering perennials.

The most 'un-American' thing we did was to plant a semicircular bed on the roadside, screening the front of the house from passers-by. Typically, the front lawn of most suburban front gardens sweeps right down to the road to link with those of neighbouring houses. Instead we planted thickly with native trees – the river birch (*Betula nigra*) and grey-stemmed amelanchier (*Amelanchier arborea*) chosen for their winter bark. Under the trees I suggested using small native American spring-flowerers and bulbs; these were later supplemented with ferns.

ABOVE *Under the trellis-work pavilions, constructed from cedar laths that silver with age, giant white-flowered* Nicotiana sylvestris, *grown from seed each year, are features in large pots to mark the end of both crab alleys.*

FAR LEFT *Looking from the glasshouse to the main sitting area, paved with green slate. On one side of the terrace, the Main Mixed Border is planted with foliage plants which look effective through the summer, even when not in flower. Tall Bradford pears screen neighbouring houses. Decorative pots are planted with tender blue and mauve salvias and silver-leaved plants. Because of the heat, they are renewed at intervals during the summer.*

OVERLEAF *The pool, positioned in full sun, is surrounded with formally laid out beds with very English planting. The pale terracotta urns are a perfect match for the slate paving.*

I was nervous about the climatic extremes when it came to finalizing the planting details. Fortunately, I not only had reference books which provided information on plant hardiness zones, I also had many notes I had made myself during previous visits to the mid-west. Of course I made mistakes, but my clients were very supportive – more than that, having become extremely interested in plants, they consistently encouraged me to experiment with subjects on the borderline of hardiness. It is satisfying to be able to note that, over the past four years and despite one very cold winter (1993/4), most of the plants have flourished. Carol Fenner, the gardener, has recommended many planting improvements and, with expert knowledge and fine horticultural skills, has been a tower of strength as the garden has developed. There are constant changes in planting nuances, always for the better, but my original design has changed little.

LEFT *In sun, white-flowering perennials including* Phlox *'Miss Lingard', white turtle's head (*Chelóne obliqua *'Alba'), Siberian iris and the spreading* Lysimachia clethroides *are backed by more substantial shrubs,* Hydrangea arborescens *and white rugosa roses. On the shady side washes of* Anemone *'Honorine Jobert',* Cimicifuga racemosa, *black-stemmed wood aster (*Aster divaricatus*) and* Geranium sylvaticum *soften the greater formality of shrub shapes. A pair of hollies (*Ilex verticillata*) frame a specimen Chinese dogwood (*Cornus kousa *'Summer Skies').*

RIGHT *Lilies used as annuals make a vivid splash of colour around the glazed pots in the box-framed beds. The flowers of* Lilium *'Scarlet Emperor' with green-tinged buds provide interest for a few summer weeks. Earlier in the season blue-flowered amsonias (*Amsonia tabernaemontana*) are massed in the beds to give a cooler effect. (See also the photograph on the title page.)*

50

A CLIFFTOP
ISLAND GARDEN

I first visited this clifftop garden on an island off the coast of Maine in North America in October 1990, having been asked by the owners to go there to review all the planting. Fortunately for me, but at that moment unknown to my clients, I had already visited the island the previous August. I had taken a three-week trip to look at summer gardens, from Long Island to Connecticut and Maine, and thence to Canada. I had visited all the principal gardens on the island, including the local public gardens, and the Asticou Azalea Garden and the Thuya Gardens on the Atlantic shore. I therefore had a list of possible plants, and my Maine notebook became my original source for the proposed new planting. Later visits to the Acadia National Park helped me to get to know less familiar native plants: the little pink-flowered native rose *Rosa nitida*, which grew everywhere, flourishing alongside blueberries (forms of *Vaccinium*), rhodora (*Rhododendron canadense*) and creeping partridgeberry (*Mitchella repens*). I wanted to use these where the more formally constructed borders faded into clifftop or undergrowth.

My clients mainly visit during July and August, and the garden was to be planned to give maximum interest for that period. 'Summer visitors' have been a feature of the island since the turn of the century, but in

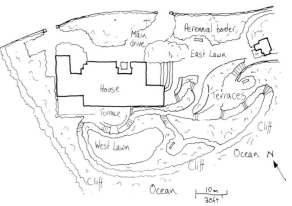

OPPOSITE Rosa '*Bonica*' and catmint mingle on the top terrace in front of an antique oil jar, with the east lawn and a glimpse of the summer house in the distance. Most of the planting in this garden is very simple, with no hint of formality. There are few bright reds or oranges in the garden as the owners prefer the gentler colours.

those grander days gardening consisted mainly of annuals around the house, with cutting and vegetable enclosures protected from wind by high cedar fences. My clients had studied the pictures in my books – both *Colour in Your Garden* and *Garden Style* – and wanted an English look, with perennials mixed with shrubs, and twining climbers on the granite walls. There were some helpful instructions about their personal favourites.

The situation of the garden was magnificent, with views to the south and east of the Atlantic Ocean peppered with small offshore islands. Warm in summer (but not too hot, and with deliciously cool nights), the area has viciously cold winters – including occasional ice storms – so the planting had to be selective. To begin with I presumed that none of the broadleaf evergreen shrubs I use so frequently in England would survive, and for safety I even chose deciduous shrubs only from a list of Zone 4 'hardies'. In fact, much of my initial caution and pessimism was soon dispelled. Because of the influence of the ocean the garden has an almost maritime climate – very different from the continental conditions found inland. Over the years we have been able to create favourable micro-climates for desirable shrubs such as sweet

bay (*Magnolia virginiana*) and *Cornus kousa*.

Moreover, even if not all the shrubs I would normally use are possible, there are compensations when it comes to herbaceous plants. With snow cover to give blanket protection, most of the familiar perennials will flourish here. Flowering clematis grow again from the base each year to make colourful additions in July and August. The spring comes late but, given rich feeding, and with long days and short nights, perennials make full use of the short growing season.

A few years earlier, a firm of landscape architects from Maryland had redefined the steeply sloping site with supporting walls of island granite, engineering a series of

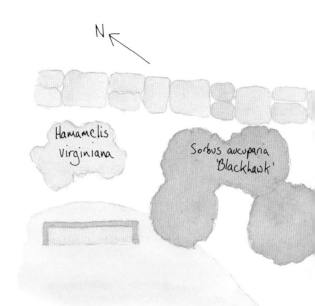

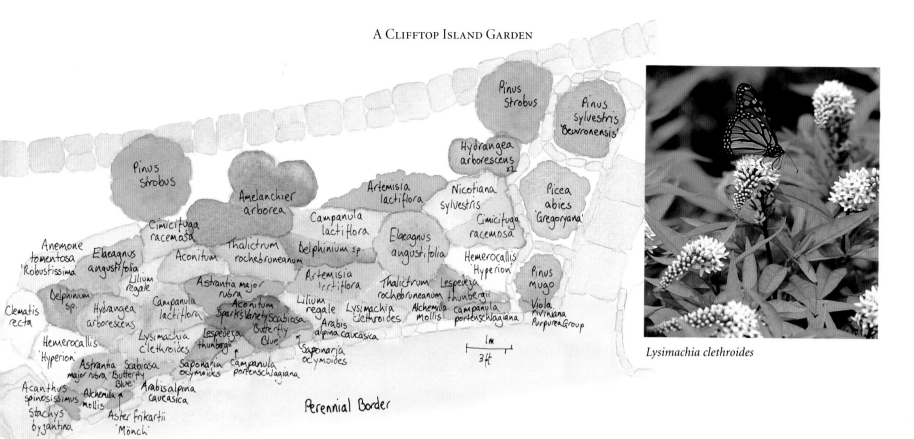

Pinus strobus

Pinus sylvestris 'Beuvronensis'

Hydrangea arborescens x2

Artemisia lactiflora

Nicotiana sylvestris

Picea abies 'Gregoryana'

Pinus strobus

Amelanchier arborea

Campanula lactiflora

Cimicifuga racemosa

Cimicifuga racemosa

Elaeagnus angustifolia

Anemone tomentosa 'Robustissima'

Elaeagnus angustifolia

Thalictrum rochebruneanum

Aconitum

Delphinium sp.

Artemisia lactiflora

Hemerocallis 'Hyperion'

Pinus mugo

Lilium regale

Astrantia major rubra

Delphinium sp.

Clematis recta

Hydrangea arborescens

Campanula lactiflora

Aconitum 'Sparks Variety'

Lilium regale

Thalictrum rochebruneanum

Lespedeza thunbergii

Scabiosa 'Butterfly Blue'

Lysimachia clethroides

Alchemilla mollis

Campanula portenschlagiana

Viola riviniana Purpurea Group

Hemerocallis 'Hyperion'

Lysimachia clethroides

Lespedeza thunbergii

Arabis alpina caucasica

Saponaria ocymoides

Astrantia major rubra

Scabiosa 'Butterfly Blue'

Saponaria ocymoides

Campanula portenschlagiana

Acanthus spinosissimus

Alchemilla mollis

Arabis alpina caucasica

Stachys byzantina

Aster frikartii 'Mönch'

Perennial Border

1m
3ft

Lysimachia clethroides

'hanging' borders linked by steep steps. These beds had been filled with good imported top soil – the soil is very acidic here and needs plenty of nutrients and annual amendment. Most beds faced east or south and had open sunlit aspects. Pockets of shade, provided by native spruce (*Picea glauca* and *P. rubens*) and the occasional white pine (*Pinus strobus* – which did not relish Atlantic gales), added interest and extended the range of plants we could choose.

On my first visit in October 1990 – for three hours and in rain – I had seen enough of the layout of the garden to do planting

LEFT *A view along the Main Border with summerhouse and spruce backed by the sky and the ocean. Cooled by sea breezes, the garden is never oppressively hot. The bright flower colour includes the daylily* Hemerocallis *'Hyperion' and, at the far end,* Thalictrum rochebruneanum *which enjoys the enriched peaty soil, humidity and cool nights.*

plans. The only structural alteration I asked for was an extension to the Main Border, which was to be edged with granite to link the planting scheme with the cliff beds across the lawn. By December I had completed detailed plans for the mainly perennial planting in most of the existing borders, and the plants were installed in the following June. I used a few native shrubs such as the chokeberry (*Aronia arbutifolia*), amelanchier, bayberry (*Myrica pensylvanica*) and black haw (*Viburnum prunifolia*). Exotics included the silver-leaved *Elaeagnus angustifolia* (Zone 3-8, completely hardy in the Main Border).

A further challenge was the planting plan for the beds supported by granite walls below the house. These were all visible from the top of the slope overlooking the ocean, slightly to the north of the house. I wanted the planting to be planned not individually, bed by bed, but as part of a whole 'hanging' scheme. Some plants could tumble down over the walls; others, supported with wire mesh,

could clamber upwards. Herbaceous clematis such as *Clematis heracleifolia* and *C. integrifolia* love to sprawl, while the small-flowered viticella type clematis grow upwards to bloom by July. To get the effects I wanted, I repeated groups of plants in some of the beds: clouds of goat's rue (*Galega officinalis*), white spires of bugbane (*Cimicifuga racemosa*), blue-flowered baptisias were all used more than once. Simple plants such as lady's mantle (*Alchemilla mollis*) and foxgloves (*Digitalis*) were encouraged to seed and create an informal atmosphere. In some areas rocky outcrops meant that planting was almost impossible, but 'native sod' containing a mixture of partridgeberry (*Mitchella repens*) and/or blueberry (forms of *Vaccinium*) or bunchberry (*Cornus canadensis*) could be laid in strips, with lilies and ferns in larger planting pockets. But otherwise the cliff planting was much like designing a horizontal border, except that the beds,

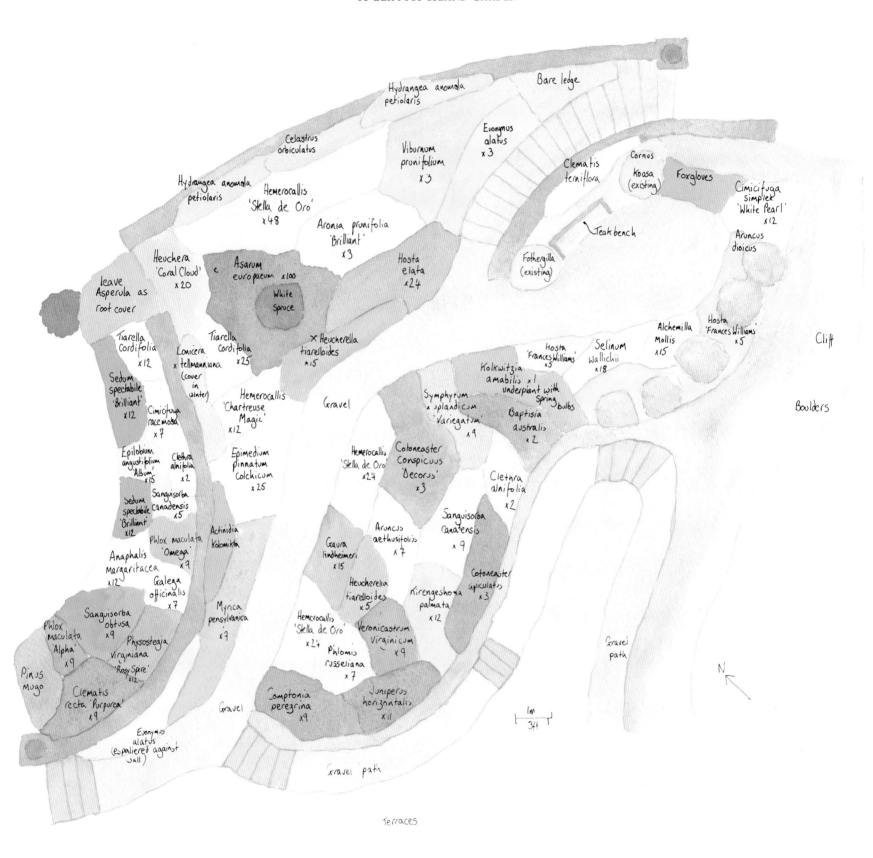

Hydrangea anomala petiolaris

Bare ledge

Celastrus orbiculatus

Viburnum prunifolium x 3

Euonymus alatus x 3

Clematis terniflora

Cornus Koasa (existing)

Foxgloves

Cimicifuga simplex 'White Pearl' x 12

Hydrangea anomala petiolaris

Hemerocallis 'Stella de Oro' x 48

Aronia prunifolia 'Brilliant' x 3

Teak bench

Aruncus dioicus

Heuchera 'Coral Cloud' x 20

Asarum europaeum x 100

Hosta elata x 24

Fothergilla (existing)

leave Asperula as root cover

White Spruce

Hosta 'Frances Williams' x 5

Cliff

Tiarella Cordifolia x 12

Tiarella Cordifolia x 25

Heucherella tiarelloides x 15

Hosta 'Frances Williams' x 5

Selinum wallichii x 18

Alchemilla Mollis x 15

Lonicera x tellmanniana (cover in winter)

Kolkwitzia amabilis x 1 underplant with spring bulbs

Boulders

Sedum spectabile 'Brilliant' x 12

Cimicifuga racemosa x 7

Hemerocallis 'Chartreuse Magic' x 12

Gravel

Symphytum x uplandicum 'Variegatum' x 9

Baptisia australis x 2

Epilobium angustifolium 'Album' x 15

Clethra alnifolia x 2

Epimedium pinnatum colchicum x 25

Hemerocallis 'Stella de Oro' x 24

Cotoneaster Conspicuus 'Decorus' x 3

Clethra alnifolia x 2

Sedum spectabile 'Brilliant' x 12

Sanguisorba canadensis x 5

Sanguisorba canadensis x 9

Phlox maculata 'Omega' x 9

Actinidia Kolomikta

Gaura lindheimeri x 15

Aruncus aethusifolius x 7

Anaphalis margaritacea x 12

Galega officinalis x 7

Myrica pensylvanica x 9

Heucherella tiarelloides x 5

Cotoneaster apiculatus x 3

Kirengeshoma palmata x 12

Sanguisorba obtusa x 9

Phlox maculata 'Alpha' x 9

Physostegia virginiana 'Rosy Spire' x 12

Hemerocallis 'Stella de Oro' x 24

Veronicastrum virginicum x 9

Pinus mugo

Clematis recta 'Purpurea' x 9

Phlomis russeliana x 7

Gravel path

Gravel

Comptonia peregrina x 9

Juniperus horizontalis x 11

Euonymus alatus (espaliered against wall)

N

1m / 3ft

Gravel path

Terraces

On one of the lower terraces, high above the Atlantic Ocean, perennials, happily snow-covered during the winter, spill out over path edges and clothe the austere granite walls that were part of the original garden engineering. Colour schemes are planned for repetition of groups on succeeding levels, with plants appearing to tumble down from one grade to another. In this area, originally shaded by a tall spruce (Picea glauca) which fell down after the first plans had been drawn up, new planting has been adapted for the increased sunlight. Cimicifuga, patrinias, a glimpse of Lonicera x heckrottii and lady's mantle (Alchemilla mollis) merge in front of the variegated leaves of Hosta 'Frances Williams', with Hemerocallis 'Chartreuse Magic' making a well of cool yellow in the background. The bushy sweet bay (Magnolia virginiana) behind the seat is wrapped in burlap every winter or it would succumb to the New England cold.

with the ocean in the background, fell down the slope.

It was a considerable challenge. I returned in February 1991 to plan improvements to the north (and extremely shady) side of the house which I had not had time to consider on my first short visit. Here we later planted ferns, ericas, local *Arctostaphylos uva-ursi* and hardy native rhododendrons (*R. catawbiense*).

Because spring comes late in Maine, June is a hectic month: winter damage must be cleared up and plant losses assessed before any new planting is introduced. Annuals are sown in March under glass, or, like tender blue salvias, pink diascias and silver-leaved helichrysums, grown from cuttings taken the previous autumn. These are used for pots outside the back of the house and also in the beds to fill any awkward spaces.

Over the years we have improved planting in the beds along the perimeter wall by the road and there has been a lot of 'tweaking' with the border plans – this sort of 'cottage-style' gardening needs annual editing. New plants have been brought in to enhance schemes, old ones discarded for poor performance or just for missing that nuance of colour that makes the picture perfect. The garden remains experimental, but always improving. I have had help from native plant enthusiasts in the planting of the clifftops and around the more formal beds, and more recently have worked with my associate in America, Nan Sinton, who is very familiar with the terrain. In recent years the experienced head gardener, his wife and his assistant, have made it possible to realize the garden's full potential.

LEFT *The view from the back of the house of the rocky coastline and the blue ocean. Pots planted with* Argyranthemum foeniculaceum *line the steps to the deck. Roses and catmint edge the lower path beneath which the land slopes steeply away.*

ABOVE LEFT *Steps lead up from the first terrace. Below the wall caryopteris and the small catmint* Nepeta nervosa *grow in close association. Both plants are renewed each season. Above them,* Clematis viticella 'Etoile Violette' *curtains the wall. Originally, this was to be C. 'Betty Corning' which I had seen in a neighbouring garden, but it was unobtainable the year we planted.*

ABOVE RIGHT *A view from one of the lower terraced paths up the steps towards the main east lawn.* Clematis viticella *'Eve', a new addition, clambers up the wall and over the neighbouring bayberry (*Myrica pensylvanica*) behind an everlasting white pea. In the upper bed spikes of blue-flowered perovskia are also new. Beyond, the yellow daylily* Hemerocallis *'Chartreuse Magic'* catches the eye and may need editing out. To the right, below the wall, you can see *Magnolia virginiana *with a group of* Sorbaria sorbifolia, *another recent addition. To the right, the sweet fern (*Comptonia peregrina*) and* Phlomis russeliana *are part of the original planting.*

COTTAGE-STYLE PLANTING IN A COUNTRY GARDEN

I began work on this garden in Somerset in the 1980s. The charming seventeenth-century stone house sits high, overlooking most of the garden, which has developed over the centuries. Many interesting changes of level give different views and perspectives from every angle and old stone walls and steps are all at different heights. Large clipped box mounds and topiary yew contribute to the garden's character and sense of permanence. The narrow terrace folding around the house slopes away at the front in an expanse of lawn, with stone steps leading down to an old wellingtonia (*Sequoiadendron giganteum*). At one side of the house the terrace broadens into a sheltered area (12 x 12m / 30 x 30ft), to the east of which, below a high buttressed wall, is a vegetable garden and beyond that a tennis court.

The owners are organic gardeners. Their very efficient and keen part-time help, Andrew Crabb, grows the vegetables, makes essential compost, and plants, mows and weeds. When I first came, there was a ground-elder problem which has been solved in the main by digging out the roots rather than by using herbicides (although I know some systemic herbicides were used in the worst areas).

There was no need for a radical overhaul of the garden – nor was this what the clients wanted – but I felt some firm structuring was necessary to balance house, terrace, garden and the intrusive tennis court. The clients were cautious, preferring gradual improvements and using Andrew Crabb to carry them out. So, we approached the garden in phases and, over the years, I have been involved in a number of different projects, taking them on one at a time, following my brief to make the garden pretty and easy to maintain.

Our first project was to improve existing planting in the double borders alongside the tennis court and to make a sitting area. I proposed an open arbour made of trellised laths, clothed in clematis and honeysuckle, to make a place to sit in dappled shade. The borders, viewed both from above and as you walk along their length, have very traditional planting – lavender, shrub roses and irises – with catmint edging both sides of the path. A few larger shrubs give strength to the design. Smaller plants, both diascias and silver-leaved stachys trail downwards on the drystone walls on the tennis court side.

Our next project was to improve the planting under the high wall of the terrace

The informal planting scheme of the double tennis court borders, looking towards the higher wall. Giant catmint lines the edges of the path, with viburnums, a beauty bush (Kolkwitzia amabilis 'Pink Cloud'), hydrangeas for late summer, and a cloud of blue-flowered caryopteris to follow on.

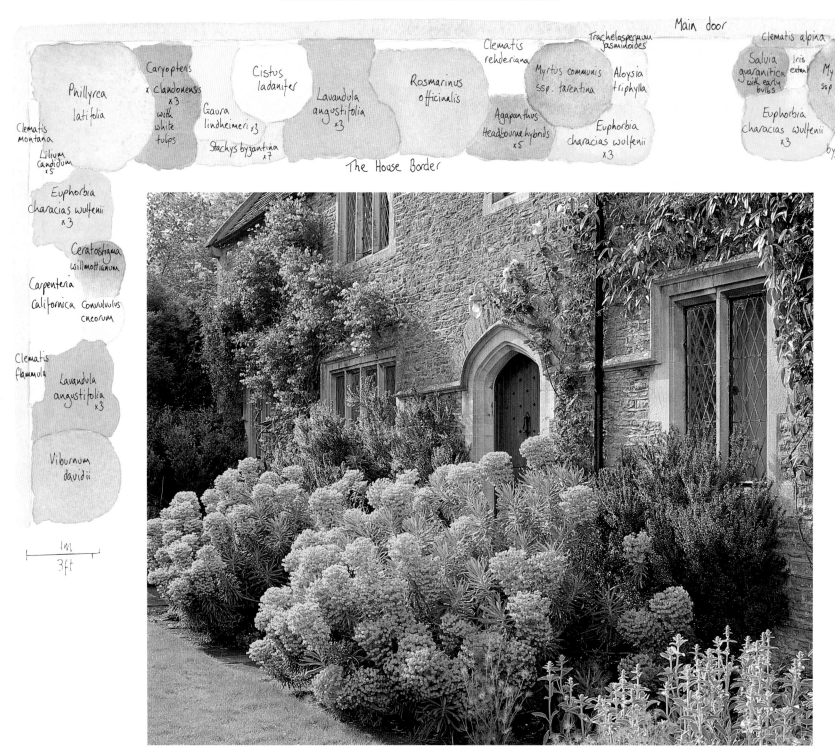

Main door

Clematis rehderiana

Trachelospermum jasminoides

Clematis alpina

Phillyrea latifolia

Caryopteris x clandonensis x3 with white tulips

Cistus ladanifer

Gaura lindheimeri x3

Stachys byzantina x7

Lavandula angustifolia x3

Rosmarinus officinalis

Myrtus communis ssp. tarentina

Agapanthus Headbourne hybrids x5

Aloysia triphylla

Euphorbia characias wulfenii x3

Salvia guaranitica with early bulbs

Iris extant

Euphorbia characias wulfenii x3

Myrtus communis ssp. tarentina

Stachys byzantina x5

Clematis montana

Lilium candidum x5

Euphorbia characias wulfenii x3

Ceratostigma willmottianum

Carpenteria californica   Convulvulus cneorum

Clematis flammula

Lavandula angustifolia x3

Viburnum davidii

The House Border

1m / 3ft

The new border under the house walls provided space for climbers as well as wall shrubs. Bulky plants were necessary as buttresses against the walls. *Large* Euphorbia characias *ssp.* wulfenii *were planted in front of old myrtles (*Myrtus communis *ssp.* tarentina*) on either side of the door, with* Stachys byzantina *spreading out over the stonework.* Clematis, *roses and* Trachelospermum jasminoides *climb on the wall behind rosemary and lavender.*

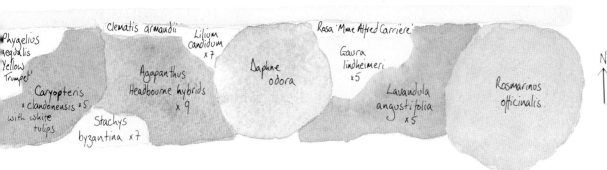

Phygelius aequalis 'Yellow Trumpet'

Caryopteris x clandonensis *5 with white tulips

Clematis armandii

Lilium candidum x7

Agapanthus Headbourne hybrids x9

Stachys byzantina x7

Daphne odora

Rosa 'Mme Alfred Carriere'

Gaura lindheimeri x5

Lavandula angustifolia x5

Rosmarinus officinalis

N

which faces east. We added evergreen wall shrubs and climbers, and strong blue and yellow-flowered perennials. Then we tackled the planting under and near the wellingtonia, with limited success because of the deep shade. Next, we were asked to widen and plant the border under the house walls, which involved re-laying the terrace pathway. I would have preferred to pave the whole of the terrace and to soften the paving with flowers and foliage falling over its hard edges. But the effect we achieved is what we wanted, with climbers and wall shrubs to clothe the house walls, large plants to provide bulk and low-growing plants to spread informally over the stone path.

Of course we have not always agreed about priorities. I wanted to have more planting near the house, and I also believed that we should start by planting in the middle foreground to hide the tennis court from the house. I suggested a pergola, running out from below the house to the wall above the

tennis court and covered in climbing and twining plants, would be effective. Ultimately we decided to replant the area, and a trellis covered with clematis along the top of the wall achieved much the same result.

Most recently, we have made a new garden outside the breakfast-room on the sheltered terrace overlooking the vegetable garden. Named as 'Villandry' after the famous French parterres, it has geometrical box-edged beds with quite formal, repetitive planting in soft colours covering the seasons. Resolving problems and understanding the wishes of the owners has worked well in this area.

Over the years I have reached the conclusion that, in general, one's first instinct about garden improvements is nearly always right, and one's immediate reaction nearly always the best. One tends to see the problems most clearly on a first visit; later, they can become blurred with familiarity and discussion. First impressions are not really 'off-the-cuff' but the result of

The border under the high terrace walls faces east. Planting includes the early-flowering lemon-yellow daylily (Hemerocallis lilioasphodelus syn. H. flava), magenta cranesbill (Geranium psilostemon), with philadelphus and clematis at the back. All the walls have been repointed over the years.

Planting under the High Wall

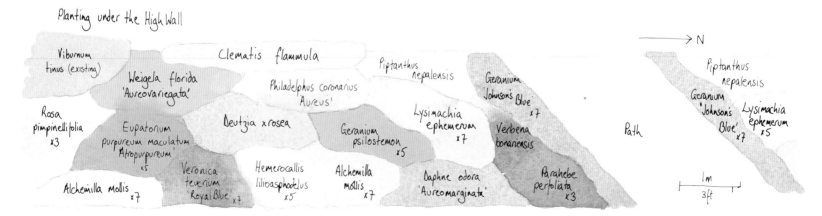

Viburnum tinus (existing)

Weigela florida 'Aureovariegata'

Clematis flammula

Philadelphus coronarius 'Aureus'

Piptanthus nepalensis

Geranium 'Johnson's Blue' x7

Rosa pimpinellifolia x3

Eupatorium purpureum maculatum 'Atropurpureum' x5

Deutzia x rosea

Lysimachia ephemerum x7

Verbena bonariensis

Geranium psilostemon x5

Alchemilla mollis x7

Veronica teucrium 'Royal Blue' x7

Hemerocallis lilioasphodelus x5

Alchemilla mollis x7

Daphne odora 'Aureomarginata'

Parahebe perfoliata x3

Path

Piptanthus nepalensis

Geranium 'Johnson's Blue' x7

Lysimachia ephemerum x5

1m
3ft

N

years of looking and thinking about principles and needs. For this garden I thought that some firm strong structuring was necessary but I have also learned that it is my task to interpret my clients' vision rather than to impose a 'right' solution; it takes longer, but the result, with clients closely involved at every step, can be satisfactory. Today, reading through my file of letters from the owners, written since 1988 when I first advised them, I can see how startled they were by innovative ideas but how, over the years, they have grown to trust me. I am grateful to them for persevering.

The sitting area on the south-east side of the house is sheltered from the wind. The 'Villandry' summer planting is restrained, with mainly blue and white flowers: here Russian sage (Perovskia atriplicifolia) and summer hyacinths (Galtonia candicans).

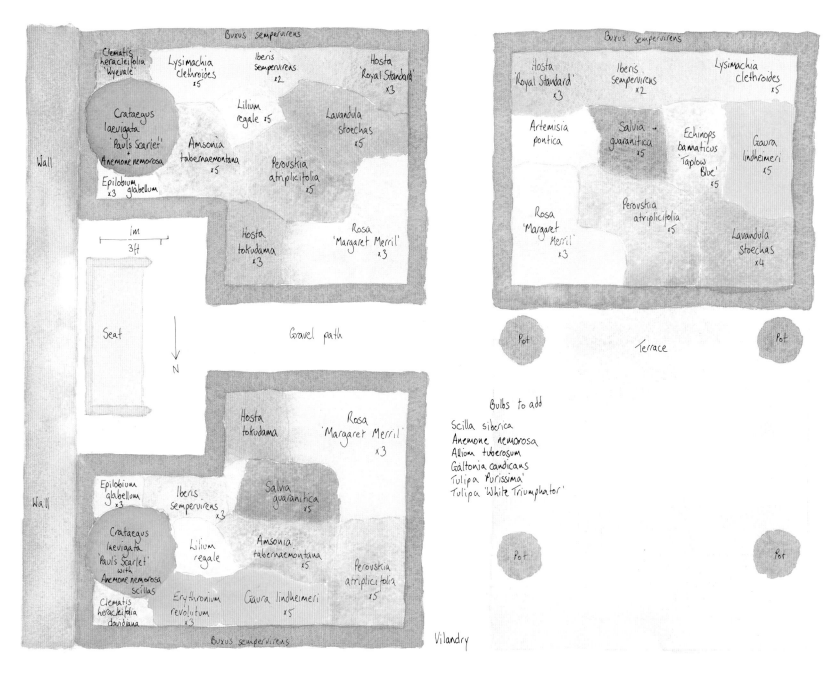

Plan labels (upper-left bed):

Buxus sempervirens

Clematis heracleifolia 'Wyevale'

Lysimachia clethroides x5

Iberis sempervirens x2

Hosta 'Royal Standard' x3

Crataegus laevigata 'Paul's Scarlet' + Anemone nemorosa

Lilium regale x5

Lavandula stoechas x5

Amsonia tabernaemontana x5

Perovskia atriplicifolia x5

Epilobium glabellum x3

Hosta tokudama x3

Rosa 'Margaret Merril' x3

1m / 3ft

Seat

N

Gravel path

Plan labels (upper-right bed):

Buxus sempervirens

Hosta 'Royal Standard' x3

Iberis sempervirens x2

Lysimachia clethroides x5

Artemisia pontica

Salvia guaranitica x5

Echinops bannaticus 'Taplow Blue' x5

Gaura lindheimeri x5

Rosa 'Margaret Merril' x3

Perovskia atriplicifolia x5

Lavandula stoechas x4

Pot   Pot

Terrace

Bulbs to add

Scilla siberica
Anemone nemorosa
Allium tuberosum
Galtonia candicans
Tulipa 'Purissima'
Tulipa 'White Triumphator'

Plan labels (lower-left bed):

Hosta tokudama

Rosa 'Margaret Merril' x3

Epilobium glabellum x3

Iberis sempervirens x3

Salvia guaranitica x5

Crataegus laevigata 'Paul's Scarlet' with Anemone nemorosa scillas

Lilium regale

Amsonia tabernaemontana x5

Clematis heracleifolia davidiana

Erythronium revolutum x3

Gaura lindheimeri x5

Perovskia atriplicifolia x5

Wall

Buxus sempervirens

Pot   Pot

Vilandry

A view from above, showing the path below the wall, a great topiary knight and 'Villandry', with mounds of box in the background. Tulips grow in the new box-edged beds in spring, with hawthorns (Crataegus laevigata 'Paul's Scarlet') to develop into broad-headed trees above the wall. Scillas, alliums, lilies and galtonias are encouraged to spread through the beds.

A Formal
Herb Garden

I n 1991 I was invited by the President of the New York Botanical Garden, Gregory Long, to redesign the herb garden in memory of Nancy Bryan Luce, 1929-87, (Mrs Henry Luce III). The New York Botanical herb garden was to contain mainly medicinal and culinary plants, but could include those used for dyes and some grown only for their fragrance. (The specific epithet *officinalis* in botanical nomenclature denotes plants with real or supposed medicinal properties; *tinctoria* denotes those used for dyes.)

The 'palette' of plants used is similar to that found in ancient herb gardens as described by Dioscorides in the first century AD, and in monastery gardens during the Middle Ages in Europe. However, by the sixteenth century European herb gardens, while still primarily 'useful', were laid out in decorative ways to enhance their whole appearance. Plants hitherto only identified and described in herbals for their functions were now appreciated for their charm and the beauty of their flowers. My design for the new herb garden only contains plants with a purpose, but it, too, is planned to please the senses and, importantly, to 'teach' the general public about plants and their uses.

A traditional herb garden is stocked with useful plants, whether shrubs, perennials, biennials or annuals. European herbs travelled, as necessities, to colonial America

OPPOSITE *A view across the herb garden from one of the seats shows how the dense planting in the fibreglass pots (ABOVE) at the corner of the central beds form architectural features. In this teaching garden it seemed important not to use many expensive 'props', and the mail-order seats are comfortable rather than luxury items. The seats are set back so that an occupant will feel the fragrant leaves and flowers are within reach. The silver-leaved pears behind the seats, planted in 1992, are just beginning to assume their mature weeping form and graceful habit.*

with the first settlers from western Europe – as did traditional designs of herb gardens. But soon indigenous American plants with curative or culinary properties, used by the native American people for centuries before European contact, were included in New

ABOVE *The common European 'holy vervain'
(Verbena or sacra herba: Verbenae) described in
Gerard's Herbal (1597) was traditionally distilled
as a treatment to bring down fevers, and was
associated with witchcraft. The more decorative
Verbena rigida, used here, was introduced from
South America in the nineteenth century and has
no recommended curative property. Domes of the
evergreen Japanese holly Ilex crenata 'Compacta'
(now I. c. 'Bennett's Compact') are planted in the
centre of each section of the knots, echoing the
symmetrical planting of taller hollies (the upright
I. c. 'Sentinel') on either side of the main entrance
to the garden.*

BELOW *Marking out the knots.*

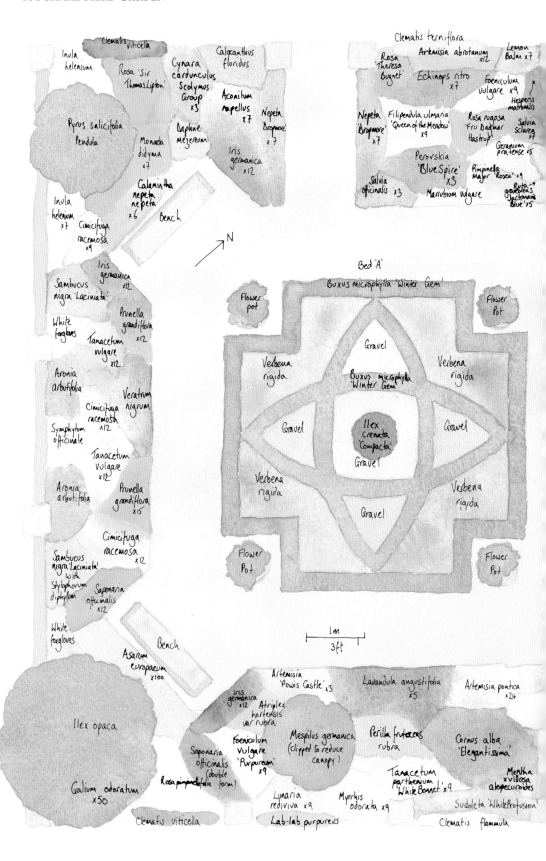

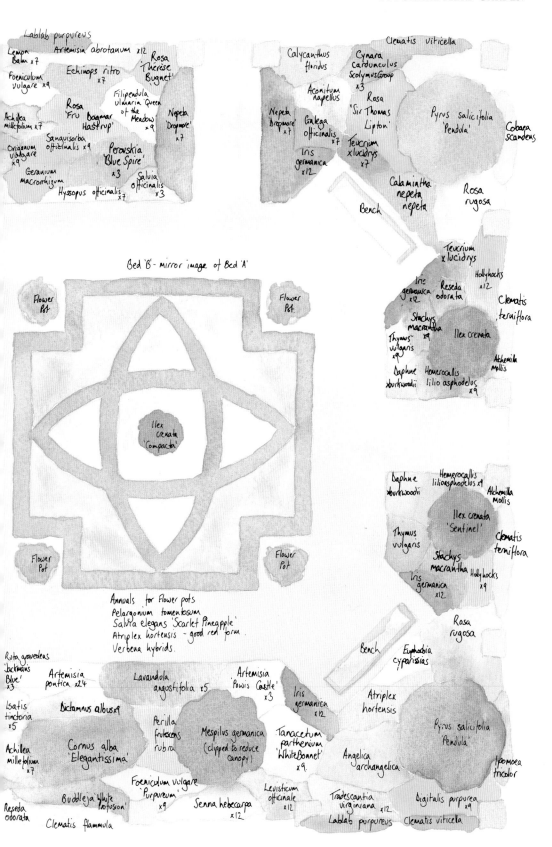

Lablab purpureus

Lemon Balm x7 — Artemisia abrotanum x12 — Rosa 'Thérèse Bugnet' x7

Foeniculum vulgare x9 — Echinops ritro x7

Rosa 'Fru Dagmar Hastrup' — Filipendula ulmaria Queen of the Meadow — Nepeta 'Dropmore' x7

Achillea millefolium x7

Sanguisorba officinalis x9

Origanum vulgare x9 — Perovskia 'Blue Spire' x3

Geranium macrorrhizum — Salvia officinalis x3

Hyssopus officinalis x7

Clematis viticella

Calycanthus floridus — Cynara cardunculus Scolymus Group x3

Aconitum napellus — Rosa 'Sir Thomas Lipton'

Nepeta 'Dropmore' x7 — Galega officinalis x7 — Teucrium x lucidrys x7

Iris germanica x12

Pyrus salicifolia 'Pendula' — Cobaea scandens

Calamintha nepeta nepeta — Rosa rugosa

Bench

Teucrium x lucidrys

Iris germanica x12 — Reseda odorata — Hollyhocks x12

Stachys macrantha x9 — Ilex crenata — Clematis terniflora

Thymus vulgaris x9

Daphne x burkwoodii — Hemerocallis lilio asphodelos x9 — Alchemilla mollis

Bed 'B' – mirror image of Bed 'A'

Flower Pot — Flower Pot

Ilex crenata 'Compacta'

Daphne x burkwoodii — Hemerocallis lilioasphodelos x9 — Alchemilla mollis

Thymus vulgaris — Ilex crenata 'Sentinel' — Clematis terniflora

Stachys macrantha — Hollyhocks x9

Iris germanica x12

Flower Pot — Flower Pot

Rosa rugosa

Annuals for Flower pots
Pelargonium tomentosum
Salvia elegans 'Scarlet Pineapple'
Atriplex hortensis – good red form.
Verbena hybrids.

Bench — Euphorbia cyparisias

Ruta graveolens 'Jackmans Blue' — Artemisia pontica x24 — Lavandula angustifolia x5 — Artemisia 'Powis Castle' x3 — Iris germanica x12 — Atriplex hortensis — Pyrus salicifolia 'Pendula' — Ipomoea tricolor

Isatis tinctoria x5 — Dictamnus albus x9

Perilla frutescens rubra — Mespilus germanica (clipped to reduce canopy) — Tanacetum parthenium 'White Bonnet' x9.

Achillea millefolium x7 — Cornus alba 'Elegantissima'

Angelica archangelica

Foeniculum vulgare 'Purpureum' x9 — Levisticum officinale x12 — Digitalis purpurea x9

Reseda odorata — Buddleja 'White Profusion' — Senna hebecarpa x12 — Tradescantia virginiana x12

Clematis flammula — Lablab purpureus — Clematis viticella

ABOVE *The decorative annual sunflower (Helianthus annuus) is used to fill in gaps between the more permanent planting. Woody sages from Europe survive the New York climate but other tender salvias, with equally fragrant leaves, are, like the sunflower, added for the summer. The sunflower was introduced to Europe from South America by the Spanish in the sixteenth century. Known originally as 'Indian sun' or 'golden floure of Peru', it grows to 4m (14ft) in one season. Both Gerard (1597) and Parkinson (1629) recommend the flower buds for eating.*

BELOW *Preparing to plant the box.*

69

England gardens. The Nancy Bryan Luce Herb Garden was to be a synthesis of both European and American cultures. It seemed appropriate to use a European consultant for what was in the main an historical concept, and I felt greatly honoured to have been asked to design it.

The New York Botanical Garden is in the Bronx, in New York City. It lies in hardiness Zone 6, so temperatures are not very extreme, although the winters are far colder and summers much hotter and drier than in the temperate British Isles. I was surprised to find that most of the herbs that I would use in England were perfectly hardy there, but because of the hotter and drier summers some of the beds have irrigation systems and all are watered regularly.

Plants for the new herb garden were propagated and grown on by the staff of the Botanical Garden, led by Michael A. Ruggiero, who also completed the layout and planting. The herb gardener, Lisa D. Cady, maintains the garden and each year adds annuals in pots and beds as finishing touches. Many traditional herbs have aggressive habits and quickly become untidy, especially in a very hot summer.

The main planting borders of this rectangular garden are round the edge. Small trees (weeping pears, *Pyrus salicifolia* 'Pendula') at each corner provide height and essential winter structure, without putting the beds in shade. In one corner an original specimen of an American holly, *Ilex opaca*, remains. Planting in the borders, although mainly of traditional sun-loving perennials, includes shrubs such as lavender, lavender cotton, rosemary, culinary sage (*Salvia officinalis*, both the golden- and the purple-leaved forms), the beautiful blue-flowered Russian sage (*Perovskia atriplicifolia*) with equally fragrant leaves, grown as a sub-shrub, and Rugosa roses. Seats under the trees make welcome resting places for visitors to this highly aromatic garden.

Using a pattern adapted from a standard Tudor knot garden, the 'looped' central beds are edged with box – a hardy cultivar of the Japanese boxwood (*Buxus microphylla* 'Winter Gem'). In 1992, the year the garden opened, we used glaucous-leaved Jackman's rue (*Ruta graveolens*) for summer bedding, alternating with gravel, between the box hedges. Recently, the more colourful mauve verbena (*Verbena rigida*) has been planted in place of the rue, which causes blisters to the skin in hot weather. Fibreglass pots at the eight corners of the knot garden, and patterned brick paths, complete the design.

LEFT *The garden needs quite intensive maintenance as many herbs seed prolifically and have untidy spreading habits. The bronze-leaved form of the ordinary culinary fennel* (Foeniculum vulgare 'Purpureum') *and common yarrow* (Achillea millefolium) *sprawl together at the side of the garden. In the perennial borders beyond, exotic grasses and perennials grow in great sweeps of colour.*

RIGHT *By late summer the Russian sage* (Perovskia atriplicifolia), *with grey leaves and pale blue flowers, is in full bloom, accompanied by silvery-leaved artemisias. Only introduced into gardens from Asia in 1904, perovskia is not a traditional herb but earns a place because of its aromatic foliage. A sub-shrub, it is cut to the ground each year. Framed by trees, the Enid A. Haupt Conservatory looks down on the herb garden. Brick paths which reflect heat were used throughout the design.*

A Garden of
Light and Shade

RIGHT *Ancient oak trees* (Quercus virginiana*)
shade the eastern end of the new Pool Garden by
the house. The open sunlit borders edging the rill
are densely planted to flower over a very long
season. This view from the arbour gives a glimpse of
the terrace on the garden side of the house.*

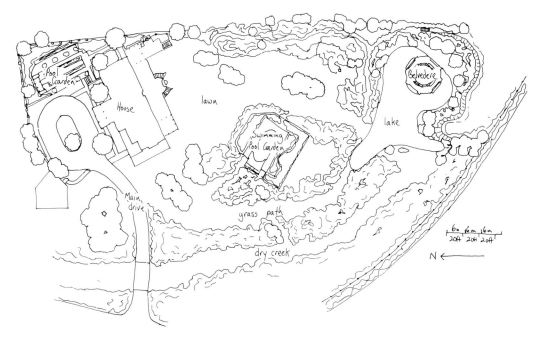

out any sub-tropical planting. The average
growing season is reckoned to be about 260
days. The soil in Austin is very alkaline:
heavy gummy clay in which plant roots can
easily rot, unless sand and gypsum are
incorporated to improve drainage and
aeration.

Existing trees and need for privacy
controlled all the design elements, and the
site and the climate dictated our planting
style. The garden was (and still is) very
green, dominated by shade-giving trees.
There were only two open sunlit areas – on
the north-east side of the house, where I
designed a new Pool Garden, and the lawn
area, sloping south from the house, where we
created shelter for the exposed swimming
pool and flower borders on either side of it.
Later, we made a lake to the south-east of the
property.

Fine existing trees included southern live
oaks (*Quercus virginiana*), cedar elms (*Ulmus
crassifolia* – a small-scale elegant deciduous
elm, completely new to me) and yaupon (*Ilex
vomitoria*, a holly for hot dry situations,
deriving its name from its use by native
Americans as an emetic after swallowing
poison). Two fine pecans (*Carya illinoiensis*)
grew on the garden side of the house. This
was my first experience of working with
many of these plants, although I had seen
examples of the oaks in some of the southern
states, and had already come to love the stiff

I first received a telephone call from Alex
Sheshunoff in Austin, Texas, in July
1990. He had been given my number,
together with that of the garden designer
John Brookes, by mutual friends. When he
rang, Alex had the two numbers in front of
him, and in fact asked for John. I said who I
was and offered to give him John's number,
but he immediately invited me to fly to Texas
and give advice about the garden. If I had
been out he would have rung John.

Alex and Gabrielle Sheshunoff, apart from
a summer break in Maine (where I was to
design another garden for them, see page
138), live and work in Austin. Their property
lies between two busy roads and the white
Texan limestone house, built in 1926 in
Spanish-Italian style, has cool shady loggias
to provide escape from the sun. Summers in
Austin are very hot and prolonged, with
warm humid air sweeping in from the Gulf
of Mexico. Heat and humidity cause many
fungal infections, as well as black aphids and
other diseases. Winters are seldom severe
(with temperatures rarely falling as low as
17°F (-8°C)) but sudden drops in
temperature, followed by warm spells, make
it difficult for plants to acclimatize, and rule

habit and greenish-grey leaves of the yaupon. A more compact form is often used for hedging. We have planted this around the base of the house terrace.

I wanted to create a garden which flowed naturally from the house, with the central sloping and undulating lawn, open and sunlit, enclosed by dark woodland. I had to work with major decisions already taken before I became involved. A new wall was being built along the roadsides to either side of the property, and the entrance and driveway were being diverted for safer and shorter access. It soon became obvious that planting for privacy and protection from car headlights at night were also essential. The week I arrived, six or seven very large live oaks, some with canopies to 21m (65ft) and trunks 60cm (24in) in diameter, were brought into the garden on large 4.8m (14ft) square tree spades. Transplanted from areas where they would have been destroyed, these trees had been saved for posterity; with the skilled use of the all-hydraulic tree transplanter, they would have a 95% survival rate. These had to be installed before the driveway and turning area near the house could be completed.

Many of the shrubs we planted to act as screens and to increase the 'green' density

ABOVE LEFT *From the terrace at the back of the house a double staircase descends to the garden lawn, shaded by two pecan trees. Large magnolias to the left were brought in to screen neighbours' houses and car lights at night. Trachelospermum jasminoides covers the wall and scrambles through the balustrading to scent the whole area.*

LEFT *Three large lemon pots by the front door are planted with tender cycads. The Mediterranean* Acanthus mollis *grows happily under the shade of the big oaks and remains in leaf throughout the year. The approach to the house and auto court is deliberately designed to be quiet and green.*

were Texan natives suited to the climate and soil and tolerant of half shade. These woody plants would thrive once their roots got into the existing soil. Carolina Buckthorn (*Rhamnus caroliniana*), desert willow (*Chilopsis linearis*), Mexican plum (*Prunus mexicana*), Mexican buckeye (*Ungnadia speciosa*), rusty blackhaw (*Viburnum rufidulum*), Texan mountain laurel (*Sophora secudiflora*) with scented purplish pea-flowers, evergreen sumach (*Rhus virens*). All would break the intense sun's glare in the Texan summer, when temperatures can soar to well over 37°C (100°F). Other evergreens included some very large magnolias, many laurels (*Prunus caroliniana*) and the beautiful yaupons. Plenty of exotics can also adapt to the trying conditions: forms of *Viburnum tinus*, *Abelia* x *grandiflora*, photinias, Japanese persimmons (*Diospyros kaki*) and Asiatic mahonias all thrive in the garden.

Shade- and drought-tolerant groundcover, including acanthus, aspidistras, liriope and salvias, was planted in great sweeps under the trees where it could spread without irrigation (the oaks are particularly sensitive to watering systems), while the native Turk's cap (*Malviscus drummondii*), much visited by humming birds, survives in the shadiest site. The grey-leaved agarito (*Mahonia trifoliata*) from west Texas, with yellow spring flowers followed by red currant-like berries, was planted as groundcover for an exposed area outside the garden walls.

The only possible places for conventional flowery border planting were in the two open sunlit areas. Even here, and also for the colourful seasonal planting in pots (from

RIGHT *Ebullient plantings in ornamental pots are planned for areas in full sun. Here, silvery senecio, rosemary, violas,* Iberis sempervirens, *pelargoniums and pansies are arranged by Jim Tolstrup, the head gardener.*

England) on the terrace, I had to learn a whole new plant vocabulary. After establishing a turning area near the house, there was space for the new Pool Garden. A narrow central rill – almost Islamic in mood – leads to a pergola arbour, covered with scented climbers. The pool is edged with thick planting to flower over a long season: verbenas, *Gaura lindheimeri*, ceratostigmas and blue-flowered *Eupatorium coelestinum* mingle with roses and gomphrenas. Tender shrubs, herbaceous perennials and bulbs enjoy the heat. Panels of lawn (St Augustine grass), planted with a rhythm of four *Diospyros texana* on each side, edge the pool, with sprawling rosemaries and roses overhanging the auto court.

We fenced in the Swimming Pool (a legal requirement) and hid it with thick planting. Lying in partial sunlight, it is now approached through dark undergrowth. Here, borders in half shade allow planting of agapanthus, *Ruellia caroliniensis* 'Blue Shade', salvias (including the shade-tolerant *Salvia regla* and *S. greggii*), bletillas, red yucca (*Hesperaloe parviflora*) and Hinkley's

ABOVE *The design of the Pool Garden flows from the pergola arbour. The position of the four piers dictates not only the width of the rill but also that of the flowerbeds and brick paths surrounding it. Scented climbers smothering the arbour include coral vine (*Antigonon leptopus*) with bright pink flower clusters, jasmines, sweet autumn clematis (*C. terniflora*), Rosa laevigata 'Anemonoides' and R. banksiae. Many South Africans, such as kniphofias, tulbaghias and crinums, flourish in the flower beds.*

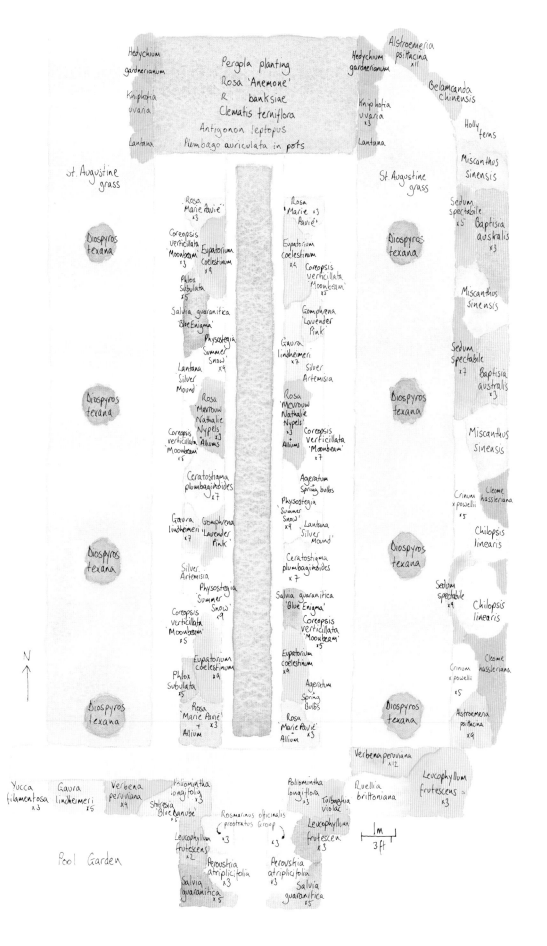

Pergola planting
Rosa 'Anemone'
R. banksiae
Clematis terniflora
Antigonon leptopus
Plumbago auriculata in pots

Hedychium gardnerianum

Kniphofia uvaria

Lantana

St. Augustine grass

Diospyros texana

Rosa 'Marie Pavié' x3

Coreopsis verticillata 'Moonbeam' x3

Eupatorium coelestinum x9

Phlox Subulata x5

Salvia guaranitica 'Blue Enigma'

Physostegia 'Summer Snow' x9

Lantana 'Silver Mound'

Rosa 'Mevrouw Nathalie Nypels' x3 + Alliums

Coreopsis verticillata 'Moonbeam' x5

Ceratostigma plumbaginoides x7

Gaura lindheimeri x7

Gomphrena 'Lavender Pink'

Silver Artemisia

Physostegia 'Summer Snow' x9

Coreopsis verticillata 'Moonbeam' x5

Eupatorium coelestinum x9

Phlox Subulata x5

Rosa 'Marie Pavié' x3 + Allium

Rosa 'Marie Pavié' x3

Eupatorium coelestinum x9

Coreopsis verticillata 'Moonbeam' x5

Gomphrena 'Lavender Pink'

Gaura lindheimeri x7

Silver Artemisia

Rosa 'Mevrouw Nathalie Nypels' x3 + Alliums

Coreopsis verticillata 'Moonbeam' x7

Ageratum Spring bulbs

Physostegia 'Summer Snow' x9

Lantana 'Silver Mound'

Ceratostigma plumbaginoides x7

Salvia guaranitica 'Blue Enigma'

Coreopsis verticillata 'Moonbeam' x5

Eupatorium coelestinum x9

Ageratum Spring Bulbs

Rosa 'Marie Pavié' x3 + Allium

Hedychium gardnerianum

Kniphofia uvaria x3

Lantana

St. Augustine grass

Diospyros texana

Diospyros texana

Diospyros texana

Alstroemeria psittacina x11

Belamcanda chinensis

Holly ferns

Miscanthus sinensis

Sedum spectabile x5

Baptisia australis x3

Miscanthus sinensis

Sedum spectabile x7

Baptisia australis x3

Miscanthus sinensis

Crinum x powellii x5

Cleome hassleriana

Chilopsis linearis

Sedum spectabile x9

Chilopsis linearis

Cleome hassleriana

Crinum x powellii x5

Alstroemeria psittacina x9

Leucophyllum frutescens x3

Verbena peruviana x12

Ruellia brittoniana

N

Diospyros texana

Yucca filamentosa x3

Gaura lindheimeri x5

Verbena peruviana x9

Poliomintha longifolia

Stokesia 'Blue Danube'

Leucophyllum frutescens x2

Perovskia atriplicifolia

Salvia guaranitica x5

Rosmarinus officinalis prostratus Group x3

Poliomintha longifolia x3

Tulbaghia violac

Leucophyllum frutescens x3

Perovskia atriplicifolia x3

Salvia guaranitica x5

Pool Garden

1 m
3 ft

ABOVE *Large-flowered hybrid clematis*

BELOW Gaura lindheimeri

BELOW Plumbago auriculata

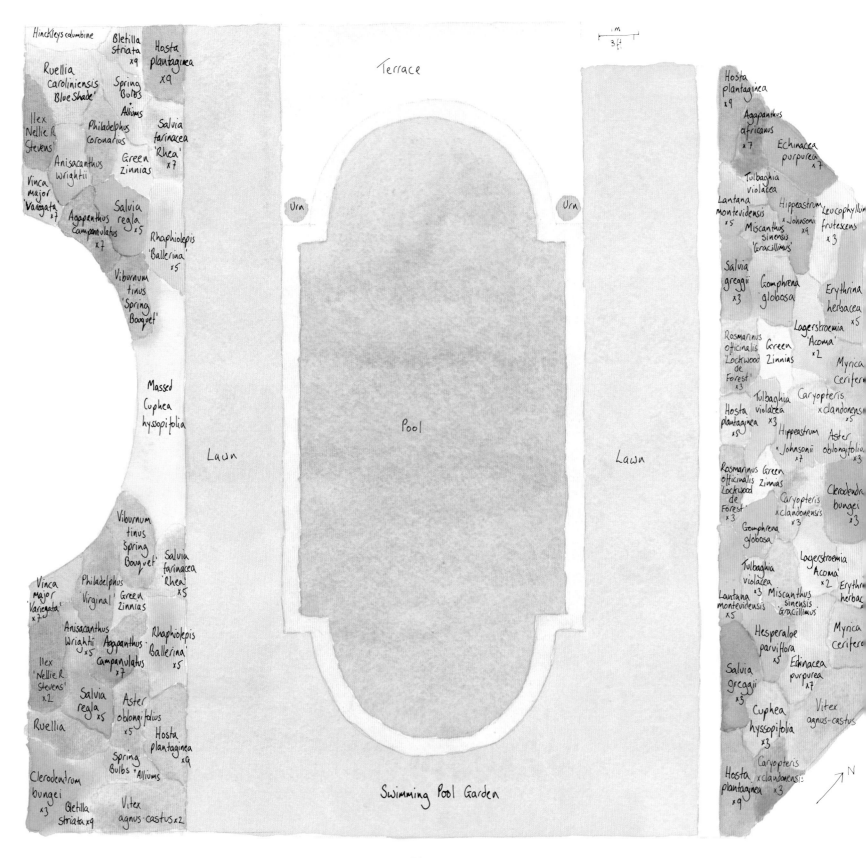

Terrace

Hinckleys columbine

Bletilla
Striata
x9

Hosta
plantaginea
x9

Spring
Bulbs
+
Alliums

Ruellia
caroliniensis
'Blue Shade'

Ilex
'Nellie R
Stevens'

Philadelphus
Coronarius

Salvia
farinacea
'Rhea'
x7

Anisacanthus
Wrightii

Green
Zinnias

Vinca
major
'Variegata'
x7

Agapanthus
Campanulatus
x7

Salvia
regla
x5

Rhaphiolepis
'Ballerina'
x5

Viburnum
tinus
'Spring
Bouquet'

Massed
Cuphea
hyssopifolia

Lawn

Viburnum
tinus
'Spring
Bouquet'

Salvia
farinacea
'Rhea'
x5

Vinca
major
'Variegata'
x7

Philadelphus
Virginal

Green
Zinnias

Anisacanthus
Wrightii
x5

Agapanthus
Campanulatus
x7

Rhaphiolepis
'Ballerina'
x5

Ilex
'Nellie R.
Stevens'
x2

Salvia
regla
x5

Aster
oblongifolius
x5

Hosta
plantaginea
x9

Ruellia

Spring
Bulbs + Alliums

Clerodendrum
bungei
x3

Bletilla
Striata x9

Vitex
agnus-castus x2

Urn

Urn

Pool

Lawn

Swimming Pool Garden

Hosta
plantaginea
x9

Agapanthus
africanus
x7

Echinacea
purpurea
x7

Tulbaghia
violacea

Lantana
montevidensis
x5

Hippeastrum
x Johnsonii
x9

Leucophyllum
frutescens
x3

Miscanthus
sinensis
'Gracillimus'

Salvia
greggii
x3

Gomphrena
globosa

Erythrina
herbacea
x5

Rosmarinus
officinalis
'Lockwood
de
Forest'
x3

Green
Zinnias

Lagerstroemia
'Acoma'
x2

Myrica
cerifera

Hosta
plantaginea
x5

Tulbaghia
violacea
x3

Caryopteris
x clandonensis
x5

Hippeastrum
x Johnsonii
x7

Aster
oblongifolius
x3

Rosmarinus
officinalis
'Lockwood
de
Forest'
x3

Green
Zinnias

Caryopteris
x clandonensis
x3

Clerodendrum
bungei
x3

Gomphrena
globosa

Tulbaghia
violacea
x3

Lagerstroemia
'Acoma'
x2

Erythrina
herbac

Lantana
montevidensis
x5

Miscanthus
sinensis
Gracillimus

Hesperaloe
parviflora
x5

Myrica
cerifera

Salvia
greggii
x3

Echinacea
purpurea
x7

Cuphea
hyssopifolia
x3

Vitex
agnus-castus

Hosta
plantaginea
x9

Caryopteris
x clandonensis
x3

N

RIGHT *The Coade stone fountain mask on the back wall of the swimming pool drips into a trough framed by tender evergreen foliage plants.*

BELOW *The Swimming Pool Garden was totally exposed but is now sheltered by thick evergreen planting of trees and shrubs. There are borders in half shade on either side. The pool surround, walls and paving are built of limestone similar to the material used for the main house. Pots on the terrace are planted by Jim Tolstrop so as to have flowers for most of the year. When the Sheshunoffs go to Maine for two summer months, Jim has an opportunity to replant all the pots and cut back many of the flower garden plants, which will flower again for their return after Labor Day.*

columbine (*Aquilegia chrysantha* var. *hinckleyana*) together with massed *Cuphea hyssopifolia* which flowers all summer and much of the winter.

The final project, undertaken a year later, was a new lake and garden building at the bottom of the garden. With architectural detail based on the Belvedere in the gardens of the Petit Trianon at Versailles, the building is surrounded by wings of water so that it appears to float. Dense planting conceals lake and belvedere from the house until the final approach, and a high berm with more thick planting deadens the sound of traffic on the adjacent road.

ABOVE *A view down the grassy rise, under oaks and cedar elms, towards the lake with plantings of flag iris. The arching oaks were acquired to create this framed view of the edge of the lake, with the belvedere hidden around the corner.*

LEFT *Planting in and by the new lake is mainly of natives, designed to give naturalistic effects. Here the contrasting shapes and habits of* Iris laevigata *and* Cyperus papyrus *make drifts at the waterside.*

RIGHT *The belvedere at the bottom of the garden – a surprise feature – seems to float on the water like the Music Temple at High Wycombe. Waterlilies make rafts on the calm surface.*

ABOVE *The view down the main south west axis of the garden leads out into the surrounding countryside, the mown ride acting as an extension of the brick and flint path.*

BELOW *In the borders along the central path,* Allium multibulbosum *and* Nepeta *'Six Hills Giant' are in full flower in mid July. Later in the season,* Eupatorium maculatum *'Atropurpureum',* Caryopteris x clandonensis *and* Anemone *'Prinz Heinrich' will dominate this space.*

A MULTIPURPOSE WALLED GARDEN

I n November 1991 we were invited to submit design proposals for the regeneration of a derelict eighteenth-century octagonal walled garden in Buckinghamshire. The house to which the garden belonged had only just been restored and the family, barely in residence, was gradually settling in and deciding how the gardens might be used.

Our guide and mentor during this project was to be Christopher Gibbs whose taste and discernment are allied to formidable gardening expertise. Though not the client, it was to him that we took our ideas, and with his help that the garden plans were devised.

Our initial brief was to think formal rather than 'gardenesque' and to recognize that the design had to strike a careful balance between the practical needs of the household and the private requirements of the family. We should provide space for fruit and vegetables, and lots of flowers for cutting, as well as places for recreation and reflection. We also had to consider the needs of the gardeners: paths should be broad enough to take a small tractor and trailer; access to all parts of the garden must be easy; and time-consuming flower gardening should be kept to a minimum.

The site itself dictated another set of practical considerations. The garden sits in a cold valley, 150m (500ft) above sea level and surrounded by steeply rising chalk ridges with hanging beech woods. This is picturesque but means that the garden is starved of winter sunlight; there are early and late frosts; spring comes slowly; and there is little autumn warmth as the low sun dips below the surrounding hills. The soil is highly alkaline and quick to dry out. So we would have to pay careful attention to the placing of flower beds, and ensure a plentiful supply of water.

The next step was to find a starting point for the design. Here, the estate archive gave us a clue: it transpired that in the 1780s the landscape designer Richard Woods had been asked by the Fane family, who owned the property at the time, to submit proposals for a general improvement of the grounds. Few of his schemes seem to have been taken up, but we did find part of a plan to divide the walled garden into quarters by means of two broad paths. This had immediate appeal, so Woods' idea was adopted – some two hundred years late.

Once this important decision had been taken, the rest of the design fell quickly into place. Four wide paths would converge on a central octagon. The paths would be backed by yew to give a firm structure, and the octagon planted with eight white-flowering crabs (*Malus hupehensis*). From here, yew arches would lead into the four quarters: the Cutting Garden, the Main Lawn, the Vegetable Garden and the Green Theatre.

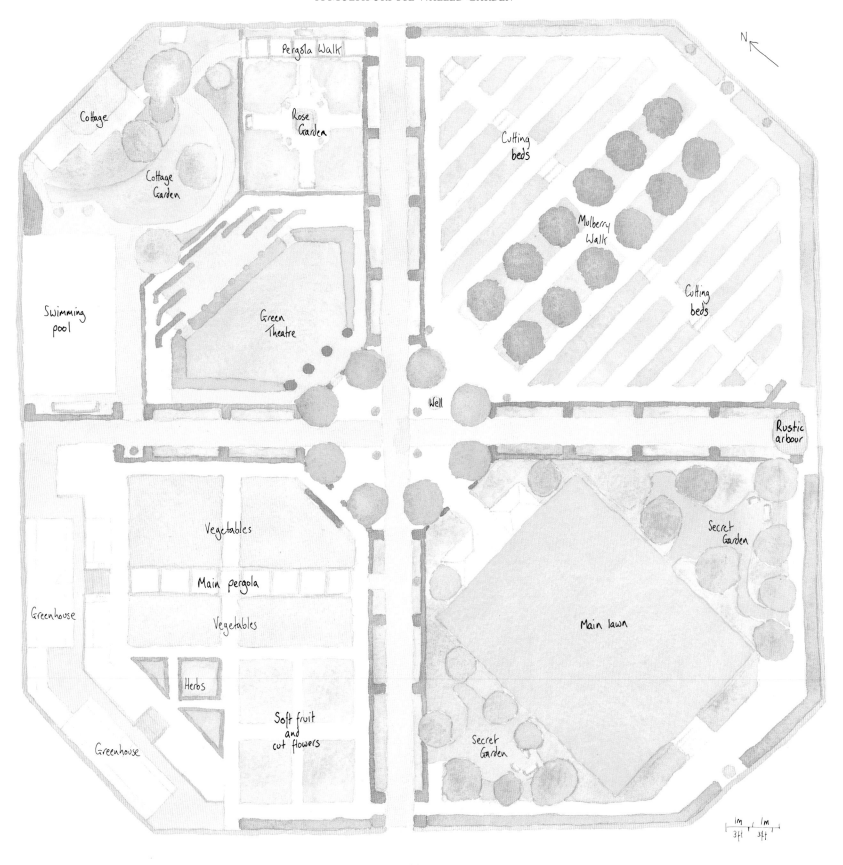

The main entrance to the garden was moved to the higher north side, and a new opening made to exploit the natural slope of the land and the view across the garden it affords. At the bottom of the garden a second opening was created, and beyond this a cut in the trees to draw the eye out into the landscape. The effect has been further enhanced by the mowing of a grass ride that runs beyond nearby trees and away to the next wood, where trees have been thinned to suggest an entrance.

The cross axis paths were built of brick and flint to match the garden walls, the narrow flint runs emphasizing their length and buttressed yew hedges creating a rhythm. The planting from the main entrance down to the orchard gate would be mainly blue, grey and white, with pale yellow, deep pink and dark wine-red accents. The path across the garden, which leads to a rustic summerhouse on the south-east side, was to have white and yellow borders.

We allowed one whole quarter for the Cutting Garden, and what seemed like an extravagant gesture at the outset has proved to be the right decision. As life in the house has gathered momentum, the Cutting Garden has come into its own, and an enormous volume of material is now taken into the house. The space was designed to be as functional as possible, with 2m (7ft) wide beds separated by broad gravel paths. An avenue of white mulberries (*Morus alba*) anchors the central axis. A colour scheme was devised that runs from white through the pastels into hot colours on the central axis, and then out into pastels again. Christopher had stressed that we should try

In the centre of the Cutting Garden, beneath the white mulberries, hot red Crocosmia *'Lucifer' vibrates in a sea of annual acid green* Anethum graveolens *sown in situ as a filler.*

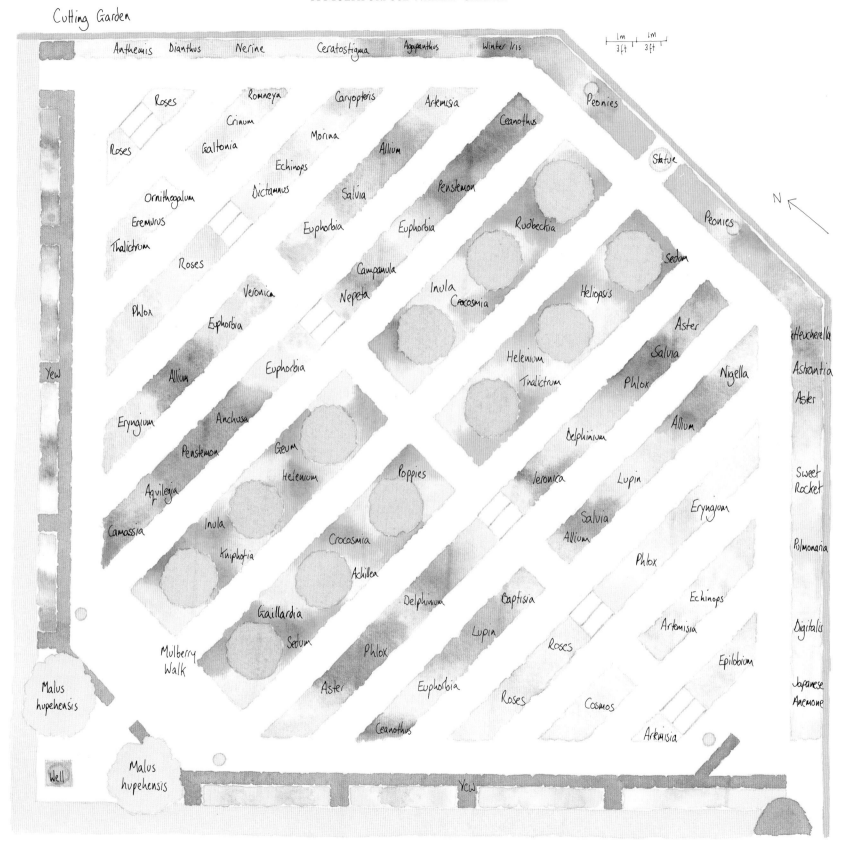

Cutting Garden

Anthemis   Dianthus   Nerine   Ceratostigma   Agapanthus   Winter Iris

1m / 3ft   1m / 3ft

Roses   Romneya   Caryopteris   Artemisia
Crinum   Ceanothus
Roses   Galtonia   Morina   Allium   Peonies
Echinops   Penstemon   Statue
Dictamnus   Salvia   N
Ornithogalum   Euphorbia   Euphorbia   Rudbeckia   Peonies
Eremurus   Sedum
Thalictrum   Campanula   Inula   Heucherella
Roses   Nepeta   Crocosmia   Heliopsis
Veronica   Astrantia
Phlox   Aster   Aster
Euphorbia   Helenium   Salvia
Allium   Euphorbia   Thalictrum   Phlox   Nigella
Anchusa   Delphinium   Allium   Sweet Rocket
Eryngium
Penstemon   Geum   Veronica   Lupin   Eryngium
Aquilegia   Helenium   Poppies   Salvia   Pulmonaria
Inula   Allium   Phlox
Camassia   Crocosmia   Echinops   Digitalis
Kniphofia   Achillea   Baptisia   Artemisia
Gaillardia   Delphinium   Lupin   Roses   Epilobium
Sedum   Phlox   Roses   Japanese Anemone
Mulberry Walk   Aster   Euphorbia   Cosmos
Ceanothus   Artemisia

Malus hupehensis

Well   Malus hupehensis

YCW

A view south across the Cutting Garden to the rustic summerhouse at the bottom of the path that bisects the walled garden. The eyes rest on the white mulberries, whose leaves emerge relatively late and are still fresh, green and glossy in late summer when most plant foliage has started to flatten out. Planting in generous swathes rather than rigid lines creates rivers of colour that run in meandering patterns through the whole area. Plenty of annuals are added so that, while providing a constant supply of decorative material for the house, the beds are bursting with colour and texture.

to plant in swathes of colour to run across the beds rather than in regimented lines within them, and that the scheme should strike a balance between the practical and the aesthetic: plants should be grown in large groups to make picking easy, and planted in drifts to make walking among them a pleasure. After two years the views across the Cutting Garden are rich in colour and texture, and flowers can be harvested without leaving gaping holes. Christine Banbury is in charge of the Cutting Garden, and we also consulted Sarah Raven, whose expertise with cut flowers has been an inspiration.

Below the Cutting Garden lies the Main Lawn. This broad green expanse, a necessary counterpoint to the busyness of the rest of the garden, is surrounded by a beech hedge and finished by two canvas tents, designed by Kenneth Topp and inspired by medieval campaign tents, that contain benches and tables. Beyond the hedge lie two Secret Gardens, informally laid out and planted.

The Vegetable Garden contained a range of greenhouses that had collapsed many years earlier. Rather than restore them in wood, we asked Alitex, who make powder-coated aluminium frames, to work with us. The result, a combination of modern technology with a traditional appearance, has proved successful, and the greenhouses allow the head gardener, Andrew Banbury, to nurse orchids and other exotics and to propagate plenty of seedlings for the Vegetable and Cutting Gardens. In the remaining space, divided by an oak pergola planted with wisteria, vegetables, soft fruit, herbs and more cutting flowers are grown.

Despite the difficulties of the site, the soil, once warm, has proved easy to work and the drainage is good. It is, however, greedy, and vast amounts of organic matter are added each year. Well-rotted manure and spent mushroom compost are preferred, but in this already alkaline soil the chalk and gypsum content of the mushroom compost has to be carefully watched. Whenever possible, it is allowed to break down before being used.

The quarter above the Vegetable Garden contains four distinct ingredients: a covered swimming pool, camouflaged to look like another greenhouse; a Cottage Garden (in front of an existing gardener's cottage); a Green Theatre and a small Rose Garden. Here, a rose-covered pergola, underplanted with shade-loving hostas and Solomon's seal, leads to seats flanked by beds densely-planted with roses, perennials and bulbs. An octagonal brick and stone pool introduces the soothing sound of bubbling water.

The structural work in the walled garden had been completed by the winter of 1992-93, and we began planting the following spring. Under the gardeners' careful husbandry, the walled garden has gradually come back to full production. It has been a privilege to be so fully involved in the resurgence of this sleeping beauty.

LEFT *A view from the pergola across the Rose Garden, looking south to the Main Lawn. This intimate area, with raised pool bubbling with water, terracotta urns filled with clipped box and handsome oak seats, is used all through the year. Roses have a short flowering season, so the planting is augmented with plenty of bulbs and perennials to create a luxuriant tumble from early spring to autumn.*

Rosa 'Roseraie de l'Haÿ'

Rosa 'Reine des Violettes'

Rosa 'Tuscany Superb'

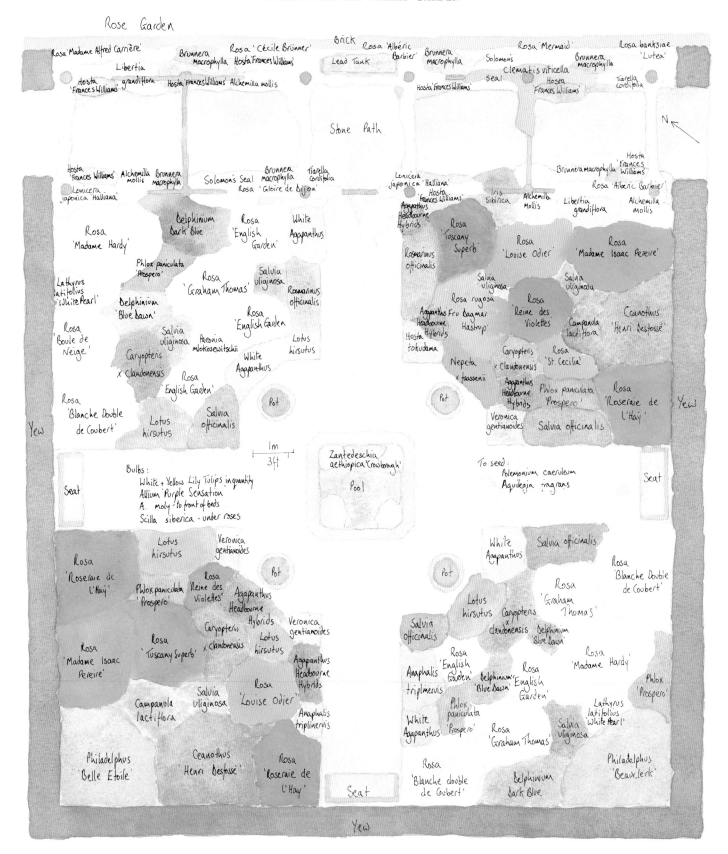

OPPOSITE *In spring the fresh green of emerging foliage acts as a welcome harbinger of summer growth to come. Clumps of euphorbia, yellow crown imperials and white tulips echo the drifts of white and yellow daffodils on the bank in the paddock beyond the garden.*

VISTAS IN A SMALL COUNTRY GARDEN

ABOVE *A view of the new bridge in spring. Grass only needs 13cm (5in) of soil to flourish, but remember to punch drainage holes in whatever base you use. Here, we faced the sides of our bridge with stone from the original bridge.*

OVERLEAF *From a bedroom window above the back door the structure of the garden becomes clear. The broad grass path, running right over the stream, leads the eye to the sundial, the gate in the south-east wall, and the paddock beyond.*

With so much of our work taking us abroad, it is always a particular pleasure to work close to home. So we were delighted when Lord and Lady Pilkington asked us to help with their garden in Somerset. Peter had retired from full-time work in London, and what had been a holiday retreat was now to become home.

Peter and Helen Pilkington had no clear idea about what to do with the garden, except that they wanted more from it. Peter expressed his vague dissatisfaction when he said that it needed 'a firm hand; making sense of'. We were conscious that we must keep maintenance to a sensible level since Helen would be doing most of the gardening herself, and while pleased to have it improved, she did not want to become its slave. Whatever extra planting we gave her should be easy to cope with: shrubs, bulbs and some perennials to add a dash of excitement in the summer.

The Pilkingtons' home is a typical Somerset longhouse of mellow stone and thatch, set in a hollow in gently undulating countryside. The house and two garden walls enclosed a lawn on three sides, and a tall box hedge created a firm barrier on the fourth. Within these confines there was little more than a mature willow, and a grass rectangle bisected by a stream that appeared from under the garden wall and wandered towards

the corner of the house at an awkward angle. A bridge across the stream was set at such an oblique angle that, from the house, it appeared rather as a barrier than as a way to the other half of the garden.

The key to our design was to unite the two parts of the garden by making a new bridge that would allow a direct path from the back door of the house across the whole space, ending at a pretty gate in the wall opposite, which opened into the paddock beyond. We decided to make the bridge flat with a grass surface. The site already had a very special atmosphere and we were anxious not to introduce anything that might spoil the sense of peace and quiet. Putting architecture into gardens requires careful thought, since any style carries its own associations, and here we wanted simply to open up the garden, not to place anything in it that might dominate or distract. The garden was to remain simple, the spirit of the place unaffected. The new bridge would look like a continuation of the path.

Once the bridge was drawn in, we moved a sundial, already in the garden, on to the main axis and created a generous circular lawn around it. This was edged in lavender. We divided the rest of the main garden into four large beds. We took the decision to ignore the stream running across the design. Whereas planting along it would simply draw attention to it, planting the beds as though

ABOVE Bupleurum fruticosum
BELOW Iris sibirica

BELOW Japanese anemone

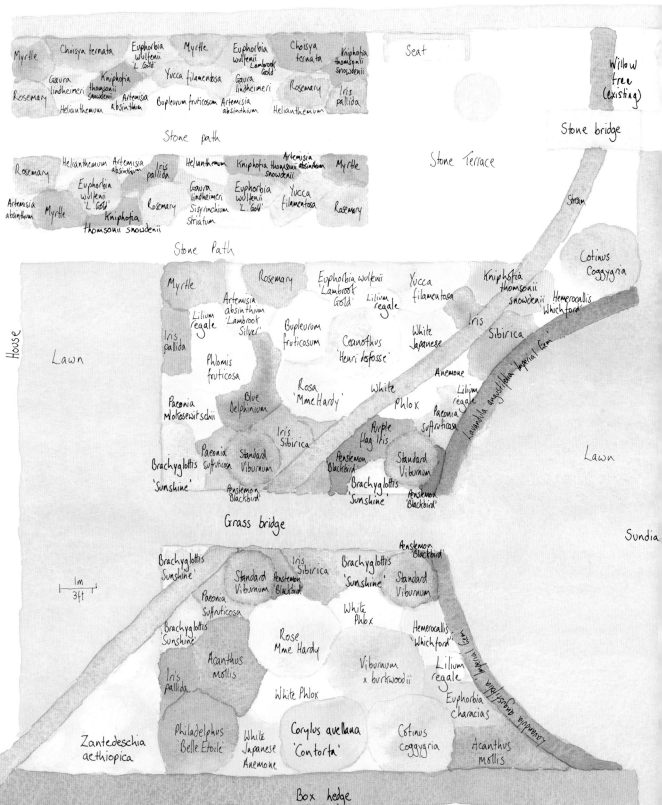

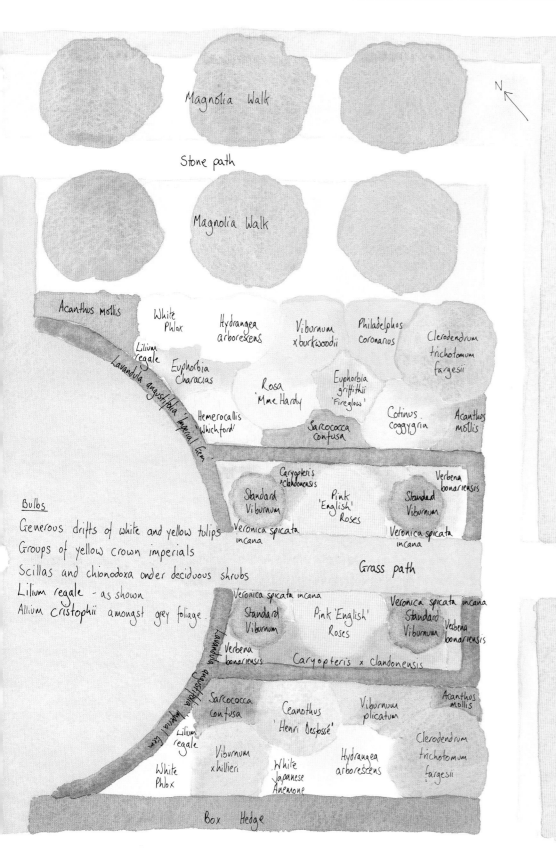

Magnolia Walk

Stone path

Magnolia Walk

N

Acanthus mollis

White Phlox

Hydrangea arborescens

Viburnum x burkwoodii

Philadelphus coronarius

Clerodendrum trichotomum fargesii

Lilium regale

Lavandula angustifolia 'Imperial Gem'

Euphorbia Characias

Rosa 'Mme Hardy'

Euphorbia griffithii 'Fireglow'

Hemerocallis 'Whichford'

Sarcococca confusa

Cotinus coggygria

Acanthus mollis

Caryopteris x clandonensis

Verbena bonariensis

Standard Viburnum

Pink 'English' Roses

Standard Viburnum

Veronica spicata incana

Veronica spicata incana

Bulbs

Generous drifts of white and yellow tulips

Groups of yellow crown imperials

Scillas and chionodoxa under deciduous shrubs

Lilium regale - as shown

Allium cristophii amongst grey foliage.

Grass path

Veronica spicata incana

Veronica spicata incana

Standard Viburnum

Pink 'English' Roses

Standard Viburnum

Verbena bonariensis

Verbena bonariensis

Caryopteris x clandonensis

Lavandula angustifolia 'Imperial Gem'

Sarcococca confusa

Ceanothus 'Henri Desfossé'

Viburnum plicatum

Acanthus mollis

Lilium regale

Viburnum x hillieri

White Japanese Anemone

Hydrangea arborescens

Clerodendrum trichotomum fargesii

White Phlox

Box Hedge

ABOVE Viburnum x burkwoodii
BELOW Rosa *Madame Hardy*

BELOW Rosa *Mary Rose*

the stream did not exist would lead a viewer's eye on and across. What had been an obstacle became an asset: the sound of water is heard as soon as you enter the garden, but the stream itself is only discovered as a surprise when you walk on to the bridge.

Peter and Helen had asked for a seating area, so we made a stone terrace just above the spot where the stream runs into the garden, and under the canopy of the willow. The terrace is reached by means of two narrow stone paths, aligned on windows in the house, and the beds on either side are filled with aromatic Mediterranean shrubs.

Our final concern was that the design was rather flat; we were keen to add verticals to the planting. However, the house sits in a hollow, and Peter rightly pointed out that in winter the sun was already low on the horizon and that trees would make the house dark. We settled for deciduous *Viburnum carlesii*, grown as standards, in pairs along both sections of the main path, and to make sure that there would be uninterrupted light, we pushed the flower beds away from the house, which now sits on a band of grass.

The garden was completed in the summer of 1995 and has just enjoyed its second full season. What had so recently been an empty space is now a heady mixture of colours and textures, with scent that carries through the air and into the open windows of the house.

TOP LEFT *The clear yellow English rose 'Graham Thomas' picks up the acid greens of* Euphorbia characias *ssp.* wulfenii *'Lambrook Gold'.*

LEFT *In midsummer, the tall spires of delphiniums are at their most memorable. In a young garden this much-loved perennial can provide instant height until the structural plants mature.*

RIGHT *On the bank of the stream, well away from the main vista, a broad swathe of* Zantedeschia aethiopica *'Crowborough' is a majestic sight in July.*

A Country Garden

with

Different Themes

OPPOSITE *The view of the lake looking over the blue and white planting by the pavilion where, in June, philadelphus and delphiniums are enclosed in box hedging. The lake settles into the landscape more each year. Grass, interrupted by drifts of planting, stretches down to the water's edge, and fussy island beds have been eliminated.*

ABOVE *Looking from the house through the white pavilion, which was already in place when we came, towards the new lime avenue and distant woods. Yews and fastigiate hornbeams mark the corners of the box hedges. In the flowerbeds, the blue and white scheme is maintained throughout the season, starting with tulips, reaching a crescendo in June with philadelphus and delphiniums and ending with summer hyacinths (Galtonia candicans).*

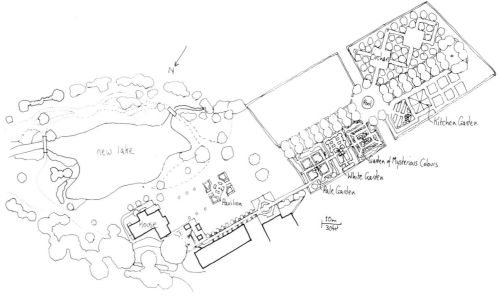

I first visited the gardens at Plön, in Holstein – one of the most beautiful areas in northern Germany – in 1993. My clients were the fashion designer Jil Sander, and Dickie Mömsen who had inherited the estate, Gut Ruhleben, from her father. Plön lies hardly 20 miles (30 km) from the Baltic and is almost surrounded by lakes. The Ruhleben land stretches down the eastern side of the largest lake and away through woods and fields to the south. With mist rising at dawn above the water, it is a peaceful and magical place.

Jil and Dickie had already established a garden around what had once been the farm's dairy house and had made a lake by diverting and damming a stream in a low-lying valley below the house. A firm of contractors had planted trees to screen the boundary and a large white pavilion surrounded by clipped dome yews had just been built on the main lawn. The garden looked manicured, and Jil and Dickie now wanted a design that would fit in with the natural wild and romantic beauty of the site.

My initial brief was to improve the planting around the lakeside, and to design new beds around the pavilion. I was near enough to Pomerania to imagine myself working like 'Elizabeth' in her 'German Garden' to bring some romantic English disorder into the tidiness. In the first year, I concentrated on eliminating banana-shaped and circular beds in the lawns surrounding the new lake, and making other plant groupings look more naturalistic. Moisture-

loving plants – Siberian iris, astilbes and daylilies – were planted in broad sweeps down to the water's edge. We added new trees in the field beyond the garden fence to disguise its harsh line and planted bulbs to naturalize in the grass.

In essence the climate is continental, with hot summers reaching 30°C (86°F) and long cold winters with recorded lows of -17°C (0°F). The soil is sandy and free-draining, very hungry and just on the acid side of neutral, though not really suitable for rhododendrons and azaleas. Frequent watering is required if there are even a few weeks in the summer without rain.

My colleague Simon Johnson joined me on my third visit, helping me design the flower borders around the pavilion and moving the domed yews to reinforce a line of mop-headed maples (*Acer platanoides* 'Globosum') that ran along the side of the barn. Box-edged beds were used to anchor the pavilion and a double line of fastigiate hornbeam (*Carpinus betulus* 'Fastigiata') helped draw the eye down to the structure and away to a gate in the hedge beyond. The beds were filled with blues and whites: massed anaphalis with 'White Triumphator' tulips, blue-grey perovskia, tall blue delphiniums and campanulas, white-flowered scented philadelphus and drifts of white regal lilies. The pavilion, which looked lonely in the middle of the lawn, is now surrounded with colours and textures and has become a favourite place in which to sit.

We also began planning a massive expansion to the south of the existing garden, where a new lime avenue (*Tilia cordata*) was to be flanked by a series of hedged gardens with different themes, but with a definite English touch throughout. Jil and Dickie's plans for the gardens were ambitious. Jil was interested in the evolution of a master plan and both of them wanted

masses of flowers. They wanted a White Garden, with more than a nod to Sissinghurst, as well as gardens using different flower colours. By 1994 we had found an English gardener, Joy Patrick, and her husband Richard, an experienced garden contractor, to be in charge of implementing our new ideas and to take over the running of the gardens. We were on our way.

Taking the gate in the existing hedge as our starting point, we designed the lime avenue to stretch some 200m (700ft) out into the field to the woodland beyond. In the middle and at the end of the avenue we broke the line with two rondels, one containing a circular pool and the other a large statue of Jupiter that had once stood in the grounds of Plön Castle. Underplanted with *Lonicera pileata* and backed with a beech hedge, the avenue links the new garden areas on either side, as well as providing a perspective view into the countryside.

On either side of the avenue we created a series of four new gardens – all secret enclosures. The first is a flower garden, divided into three, the second a vegetable, fruit and cutting garden, the third an ornamental orchard and the fourth was to have a central canal, topiary and shrub borders. Because Jil and Dickie had asked specifically for a White Garden, we decided to further differentiate our three flower gardens according to colour: pale, white and 'rich'. A firm structure of brick paths, iron gazebos, limestone urns and yew and holly topiary unites all three.

In the Pale Garden, *Crataegus crus-galli*

A view south along the wall which separates the lawn garden from thatched barn and the courtyard behind. We reinforced the avenue of mop-headed maples, planted before we came, by moving the evergreen yew domes from the lawn to line this pathway to the Pale Garden.

The view from the edge of the lawn, looking through an archway in the beech hedge into the north-west corner of the Pale Garden. A hoggin path, cross-banded with granite setts, leads to the brick paving and change of scene from shade to sunlight. The urn is framed by catmint (Nepeta 'Six Hills Giant'), pale blue Iris sibirica *and* Geranium x magnificum.

Pale Garden

Beech Hedge

Ilex x meserveae x7

Elaeagnus umbellata x2

Rosa xanthina hugonis

Yew

Crataegus crus-galli with Ajuga reptans

Iris sibirica pale blue form x12

Yew

Artemisia 'Powis Castle'

Rosa 'Madame Pierre Oger'

Anemone x hybrida 'Queen Charlotte'

Nepeta 'Six Hills Giant'

Rosa 'Complicata'

Yew

Nepeta 'Six Hills Giant'

Iris sibirica dark blue form

Dicentra spectabilis x12

Artemisia 'Powis Castle' x3

Lavandula angustifolia x8

Hosta
Philadelphus fortunei var. albopicta x9

Rosa 'Felicia' x3 with Geranium x oxonianum 'Wargrave Pink'

Prunus 'Shirotae'

Anemone x hybrida 'Queen Charlotte' x5

Artemisia 'Powis Castle' x2

Campanula lactiflora x9

Gaura lindheimeri x7

Rosa 'Gruss an Aachen' x3

Salvia uliginosa

Rosa 'Albertine'

Prunus 'Spire'

Prunus 'Spire'

Rosa 'President de Seze'

Prunus 'Spire'

Lavandula angustifolia

1m / 3ft

Prunus 'Spire'

Rosa 'Mousseline'

Prunus 'Spire'

Pink Phlox x5

Rosa 'despreza Fleurs Jaunes'

Rosa 'Graham Thomas' x3

Salvia uliginosa x5

Artemisia 'Powis Castle' x3

Campanula lactiflora x9

Yew

Rosa 'Penelope' x3 with Geranium 'Johnson's Blue'

Prunus 'Shirotae'

Rosa 'Heritage' x8 with Geranium himalayense

Lavandula angustifolia x8

Anemone x hybrida 'Queen Charlotte' x5

Gaura lindheimeri x5

Artemisia 'Powis Castle' x3

Iris sibirica dark blue form x9

Nepeta 'Six Hills Giant'

Crataegus crus-ga

Crataegus crus-galli with Ajuga reptans

Ilex x meserveae x7

Rosa 'Buff Beauty' x3

Yew

Elaeagnus umbellata x3

Philadelphus crus-ga 'Beauclerk'

Anemone x hybrida 'Queen Charlotte' x15

104

Ilex × meserveae ×9

Rosa xanthina hugonis

Elaeagnus umbellata ×3

Crataegus crus-galli with Ajuga reptans

Artemisia 'Powis Castle'

Yew

Iris sibinc. pale blue form

Rosa 'Président de Seze'

Anemone × hybrida ×9 'Queen Charlotte'

Rosa 'Madame Pierre Oger'

Geranium × Magnificum ×9

Urn

Nepeta 'Six Hills Giant'

Geranium × magnificum ×11

Nepeta 'Six Hills Giant'

Salvia uliginosa ×5

Dicentra spectabilis ×9

Hosta fortunei albopicta ×9

Rosa 'Nevada'

Lavandula angustifolia ×8

Prunus 'Shirotae'

Rosa 'Penelope' with Geranium 'Johnson's Blue'

Rosa 'Graham Thomas' ×3

Philadelphus insignis

Rosa 'Empress Josephine' ×3

Anemone × hybrida 'Queen Charlotte' ×7

Gaura lindheimeri ×7

Campanula lactiflora ×7

Artemisia 'Powis Castle' ×3

Rosa Weetwood

Prunus 'Spire'

Pink Phlox ×5

Prunus 'Spire'

Rosa 'Mousseline'

Prunus 'Spire'

Rosa 'Cantabrigiensis'

N →

Prunus 'Spire'

Lavandula angustifolia

Prunus 'Spire'

Rosa 'Général Kléber'

Prunus 'Spire'

Rosa 'Madame Pierre Oger'

Hippophaë rhamnoides mixed with

Rosa 'Mme. Grégoire Staechelin'

Salvia uliginosa ×9

Artemisia 'Powis Castle' ×3

Pink Phlox ×7

Prunus 'Shirotae'

Hosta fortunei albopicta ×9

Rosa 'Wolley-Dod'

Lavandula angustifolia ×8

Rosa 'Heritage' ×6 with Geranium himalayense

Artemisia 'Powis Castle' ×2

Rosa 'Felicia' ×3 with Geranium × oxonianum 'Wargrave Pink'

Gaura lindheimeri ×9

Geranium × magnificum ×11

Urn

Elaeagnus umbellata ×3

Nepeta 'Six Hills Giant'

Rosa 'Nevada'

Nepeta 'Six Hills Giant'

Rosa 'Fantin-Latour' ×3

Yew

Rosa 'Buff Beauty' ×3

Iris sibirica Pale blue ×7

Crataegus crus-galli with Ajuga reptans

Ilex × meserveae ×5

Elaeagnus umbellata ×5

Beech Hedge

In the Pale Garden, looking back towards the wall and lawn area, catmint spills over the brick paths and almost smothers the Bourbon rose 'Madame Pierre Oger', which flowers early and again later. Bold foliage plants are essential elements as companions to pale flowers.

ABOVE *The White Garden, although less formally arranged than that at Sissinghurst, was inspired by it. Silvery artemisias weave between Siberian iris and white roses around the box-edged beds which have taken the place of the camomile squares originally planned on the corners. Tall hollies and a background of weeping pears (*Pyrus salicifolia *'Pendula') give permanent vertical height and a three-dimensional effect which is enhanced by tall flowering perennials like the giant crambes and delphiniums and crabs (*Malus *'Snowdrift') in their season. Here, as in all three flower gardens, Joy Patrick mulches constantly with spent hops, farmyard manure and compost.*

OPPOSITE *Spires of white delphiniums are a highlight in June and July, growing as Vita Sackville-West loved them, against a background of dark yew.*

and *Prunus* 'Shirotae' anchor the corners and provide height in the main beds. Beneath the trees and around the gazebo, catmint, lavender and tender perennials such as *Salvia uliginosa* and *Gaura lindheimeri* spill across the paths.

In the White Garden, inspired by Sissinghurst, eight *Malus* 'Snowdrift' frame the garden. Three weeping pears (*Pyrus salicifolia* 'Pendula') provide a screen for a bench. Around the trees philadelphus, giant crambe, roses, iris, Japanese anenome and phlox offer a range of shades from soft cream to blue-white.

The third garden – a combination of deep pinks, dark purples and rich reds – we eventually called the Garden of Mysterious Colours. It proved the most challenging. Heavy purple foliage of *Cotinus coggygria* 'Velvet Cloak' is offset by the silver-grey of *Elaeagnus angustifolia*. The roses here are sumptuous: 'Mme Isaac Pereire', 'Tuscany Superb', 'Arthur de Sansal', 'Tour de Malakoff', 'Cardinal de Richelieu' – all names to conjure with. Peonies, geraniums, dicentras, phlomis physostegia and sedum contribute to the luxuriant mixture.

The garden to the south-east of the flower gardens is still to be resolved; our plans for a canal were too elaborate but a green maze remains a possibility. The orchard beyond has mown paths between platts of rougher grass with trees maturing and bearing fruit. The Kitchen Garden to the south west beyond the pool, produces an abundance of soft fruit, vegetables and cutting flowers.

Apart from problems with moles, a protected species in Germany (everything, including battery-operated bleepers, has been tried but with little success), working at Plön for clients who are interested and imaginative, on a site that refreshes the senses, and with expert gardeners, has brought us a lot of pleasure.

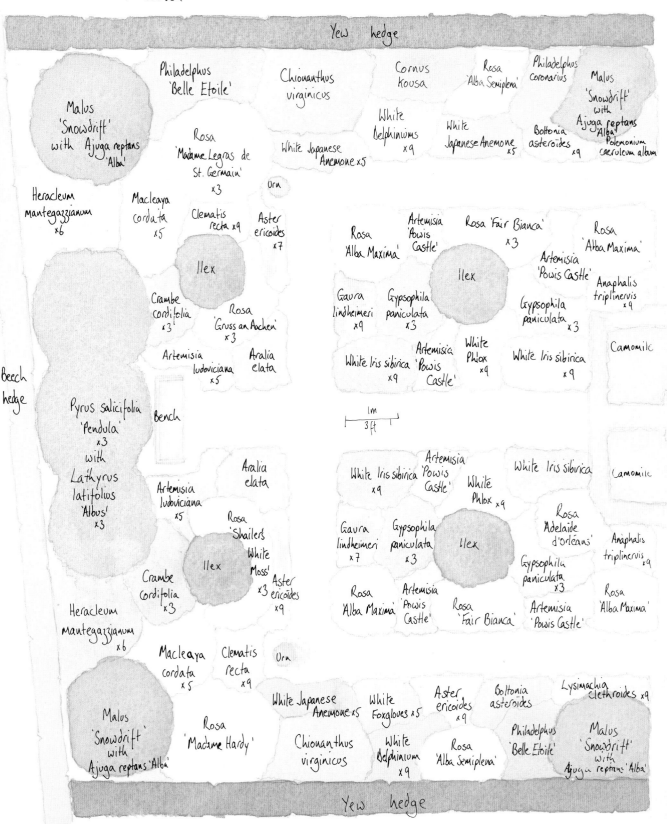

Yew hedge

Malus 'Snowdrift' with Ajuga reptans 'Alba'

Philadelphus 'Belle Etoile'

Chionanthus virginicus

Cornus kousa

Rosa 'Alba Semiplena'

Philadelphus coronarius

Malus 'Snowdrift' with Ajuga reptans 'Alba'

White Delphiniums x9

White Japanese Anemone x5

Boltonia asteroides x9

Polemonium caeruleum album

White Japanese Anemone x5

Rosa 'Madame Legras de St. Germain' x3

Heracleum mantegazzianum x6

Macleaya cordata x5

Clematis recta x9

Urn

Aster ericoides x7

Ilex

Rosa 'Alba Maxima'

Artemisia 'Powis Castle'

Rosa 'Fair Bianca' x3

Rosa 'Alba Maxima'

Artemisia 'Powis Castle'

Anaphalis triplinervis x9

Gaura lindheimeri x9

Gypsophila paniculata x3

Ilex

Gypsophila paniculata x3

Crambe cordifolia x3

Rosa 'Gruss an Aachen' x3

White Iris sibirica x9

Artemisia 'Powis Castle'

White Phlox x9

White Iris sibirica x9

Camomile

Artemisia ludoviciana x5

Aralia elata

Beech hedge

Pyrus salicifolia 'Pendula' x3 with Lathyrus latifolius 'Albus' x3

Bench

1m / 3ft

Camomile

Artemisia ludoviciana x5

Aralia elata

White Iris sibirica x9

Artemisia 'Powis Castle'

White Phlox x9

White Iris sibirica

Rosa 'Shailer's White Moss' x3

Gaura lindheimeri x7

Gypsophila paniculata x3

Ilex

Rosa 'Adelaide d'Orléans'

Gypsophila paniculata x3

Anaphalis triplinervis x9

Crambe Cordifolia x3

Ilex

Aster ericoides x9

Rosa 'Alba Maxima'

Artemisia 'Powis Castle'

Rosa 'Fair Bianca'

Artemisia 'Powis Castle'

Rosa 'Alba Maxima'

Heracleum mantegazzianum x6

Macleaya cordata x5

Clematis recta x9

Urn

White Japanese Anemone x5

White Foxgloves x5

Aster ericoides x9

Boltonia asteroides

Lysimachia clethroides x9

Malus 'Snowdrift' with Ajuga reptans 'Alba'

Rosa 'Madame Hardy'

Chionanthus virginicus

White Delphinium x9

Rosa 'Alba Semiplena'

Philadelphus 'Belle Etoile'

Malus 'Snowdrift' with Ajuga reptans 'Alba'

Yew hedge

Rosa 'Iceberg' and Alchemilla mollis

Chionanthus virginicus

Yew hedge

Malus 'Snowdrift' with Ajuga reptans 'Alba'

White Delphiniums x9

Rosa 'Winchester Cathedral' x6

Cornus kousa

Bench

Crambe cordifolia x3

Lysimachia clethroides x5

Philadelphus 'Erectus'

Rosa 'Alba Semiplena'

Rosa 'Yvonne Rabier' x6

Lysimachia clethroides x5

Bench

Malus 'Snowdrift' with Ajuga reptans 'Alba'

Hippophae rhamnoides x3 with White Clematis x2

Rosa 'Alba Maxima'

Geranium clarkei 'Kashmir White'

Rosa 'Winchester Cathedral' x3

Standard Hydrangea paniculata 'Grandiflora'

Iris albicans x9

Rosa 'Iceberg' x10

Rosa 'Iceberg' x10

Rosa 'Yvonne Rabier' x5

Crambe cordifolia x3

Anaphalis triplinervis x9

White Phlox x9

Hosta sieboldii x6

Camomile

Stachys byzantina 'Cotton Boll' x15

Cornus alternifolia 'Argentea'

Underplant all four beds with Alchemilla mollis

Elaeagnus augustifolia

Beech hedge

Camomile

Stachys byzantina 'Cotton Boll' x15

Cornus alternifolia 'Argentea'

Hosta sieboldii x6

Crambe cordifolia x3

Anaphalis triplinervis x9

White Phlox x9

Standard Hydrangea paniculata 'Grandiflora'

Iris albicans x9

Rosa 'Iceberg' x10

Rosa 'Iceberg' x10

Rosa 'Alba Maxima'

Geranium clarkei 'Kashmir White'

Rosa 'Winchester Cathedral' x3

Rosa 'Yvonne Rabier'

N

Hippophae rhamnoides x3 with White Clematis

Polemonium caeruleum album

Rosa 'Winchester Cathedral' x6

Bench

Hosta 'Royal Standard' x20

Bench

Malus 'Snowdrift' with Ajuga reptans 'Alba'

Rosa 'Fair Bianca' x3

White Foxgloves

Crambe cordifolia

Philadelphus 'Erectus'

Rosa 'Alba Semiplena'

Rosa pimpinellifolia 'Double White'

White Foxgloves

Malus 'Snowdrift' with Ajuga reptans 'Alba'

Yew hedge

Delphinium *Sandpiper*

Iris sibirica

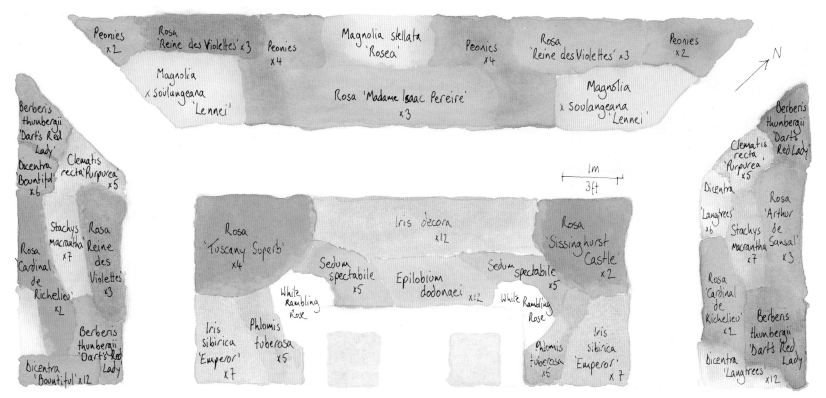

Peonies
x2

Rosa
'Reine des Violettes' x3

Peonies
x4

Magnolia stellata
'Rosea'

Peonies
x4

Rosa
'Reine des Violettes' x3

Peonies
x2

N

Magnolia
x soulangeana
'Lennei'

Rosa 'Madame Isaac Pereire'
x3

Magnolia
x soulangeana
'Lennei'

Berberis
thunbergii
'Dart's Red
Lady'

Clematis
recta 'Purpurea'
x5

Dicentra
'Bountiful'
x6

Berberis
thunbergii
'Dart's Red Lady'

Clematis
recta
'Purpurea'
x5

Dicentra
'Langtrees'
x6

1m
3ft

Rosa
'Tuscany Superb'
x4

Iris decora
x12

Rosa
'Sissinghurst
Castle'
x2

Rosa
'Arthur
de Sansal'
x3

Stachys
macrantha
x7

Rosa
'Cardinal
de
Richelieu'
x2

Stachys
macrantha
x7

Rosa
Reine
des
Violettes
x3

Sedum
spectabile
x5

Epilobium
dodonaei
x12

Sedum
spectabile
x5

Rosa
'Cardinal
de
Richelieu'
x2

White
Rambling
Rose

White Rambling
Rose

Berberis
thunbergii
'Dart's Red
Lady'

Iris
sibirica
'Emperor'
x7

Phlomis
tuberosa
x5

Phlomis
tuberosa
x5

Iris
sibirica
'Emperor'
x7

Berberis
thunbergii
'Dart's Red
Lady'

Dicentra
'Bountiful' x12

Dicentra
'Langtrees'
x12

Part of the Garden of Mysterious Colours

LEFT *Looking across the Garden of Mysterious Colours through the elegant gazebos designed by Simon Johnson, which in future years will be curtained with climbers (this is only the second season for this garden). Stachys macrantha props up the sprawling herbaceous clematis (C. recta) with irises, lychnis and roses. Dark purples, deep reds and bronze foliage plants pull this garden together, to make a contrast with the White and Pale Gardens beyond. Eighteenth-century limestone urns provide architectural definition to the loose planting in the Pale Garden and here in the Garden of Mysterious Colours.*

RIGHT Rosa *'Reine Victoria'*

FAR RIGHT Rosa *'Souvenir du Docteur Jamain'*

ABOVE *The Arrival Courtyard is treated formally with beds edged in hardy box (*Buxus *'Winter Gem') and four elegant* Chionanthus retusus.

BELOW *The two axial cross walks are planted to be at their best in spring and autumn. A pair of Japanese lilac (*Syringa reticulata*) frame a terracotta finial.*

A GARDEN OF CLASSICAL SYMMETRY

In the autumn of 1994 we were asked to help with the garden of a newly refurbished neo-Georgian house in Connecticut. Only 30 miles (48km) from New York City, and popular with commuters, the region is heavily wooded and surprisingly rural, but building is going on apace and land is now at a premium. We were therefore pleased to find that the site was a generous one: a gently rising slope surrounded by trees, with views across marshland to a mature white oak (*Quercus alba*). There were still some traces of the original forest cover, and two majestic tulip trees (*Liriodendron tulipifera*), several sugar maples (*Acer saccharum*) and a stand of white birch (*Betula papyrifera*) immediately caught the eye. Here was an opportunity to make a garden whose proportions would do justice to the house it was to surround.

The climate in this part of New England can be demanding. It lies in hardiness zone 5, and temperatures can swing from an extreme of -25°C (-10°F) in winter, with an average snowfall of 75cm (30in), to a summer high of 32°C (90°F) with high humidity. The immediate result of this is to deprive the gardener of the broad-leaved evergreen shrubs which in gentler climates form the backbone to most compositions. The ground will freeze to a depth of 60cm (24in), preventing moisture from reaching root systems, and if warm winter sun makes

plants transpire, foliage will 'burn'. Freezing and thawing can also result in plants being heaved out of the ground, and mulch is applied to try to keep the ground frozen and temperatures constant. South-facing walls, usually so welcome, consequently present the greatest problem, and most climbers have to be sheltered from the winter sun on north or east walls. Nan Sinton, our American associate, has been invaluable in guiding us through these anomalies and in helping us find plants that will do the job we ask of them in these unfamiliar conditions.

Taking the house as a starting point, we established a garden of strong axial lines running out into the landscape. The main rooms of the house face north across a lawn and down to wetlands beyond. We left this view as it was, but framed it with a pair of zelkovas and a double avenue of the early flowering shad bush (*Amelanchier canadensis*) and the Chinese dogwood (*Cornus kousa*). The double *allées* on either side of the lawn lead to finials in creamy terracotta, made, as are all the pots, by Philip Thomason in England. As in many of our designs, pots with seasonally changing displays are important, and here in New England the empty pots take on a sculptural role in winter.

On the west of the house an orangery had been built, and we took the opportunity to include a Sunken Flower Garden in our

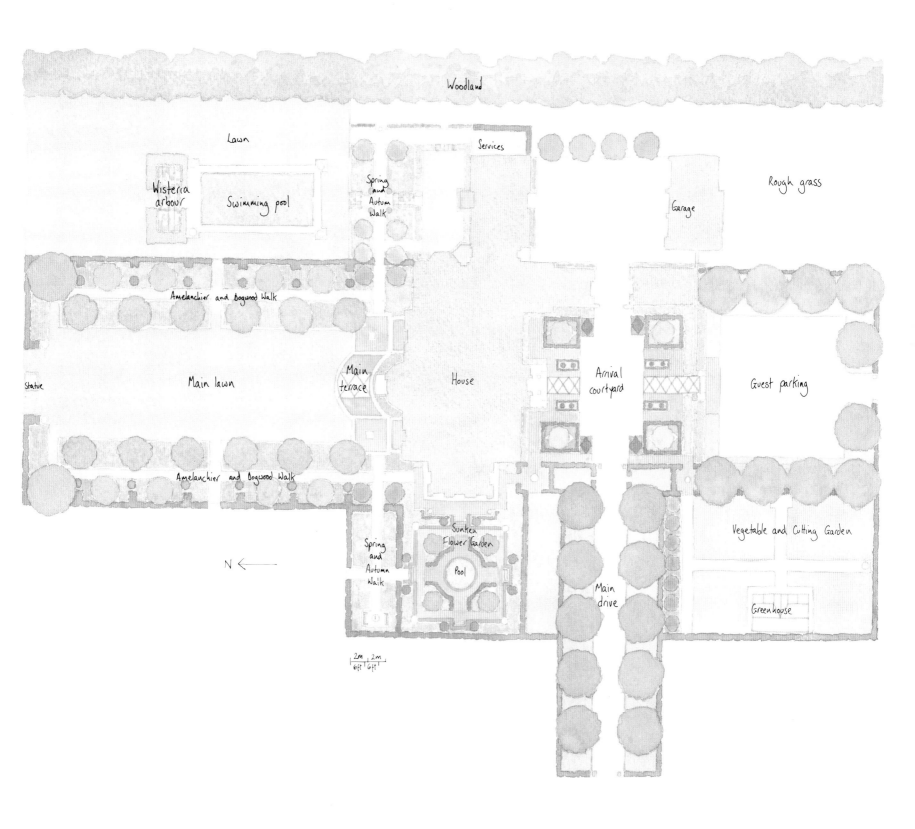

Woodland

Lawn

Wisteria arbour

Swimming pool

Services

Spring and Autumn Walk

Rough grass

Garage

Amelanchier and Dogwood Walk

Statue

Main lawn

Main terrace

House

Arrival courtyard

Guest parking

Amelanchier and Dogwood Walk

Spring and Autumn Walk

Sunken Flower Garden

Pool

Main drive

Vegetable and Cutting Garden

Greenhouse

N ←

| 2m | 2m |
| 6ft | 6ft |

scheme. Here we could grow some of the tender perennials and annuals that enjoy the hot summers. The planting is in shades of blue, grey, purple and pale pink, with massed tulips – creamy-white 'Ivorine' and dark purple 'Queen of Night' – for a more formal effect in spring . We again included a strong architectural component, edging beds in box (*Buxus* 'Green Velvet') and using box topiary to anchor the main axes of the composition. In the centre of the garden, our plan for a sunken pool was altered to a raised one to accommodate an underground power cable. Four crab apples (*Malus* 'Snowdrift') were added to frame the scene.

Spring and autumn are particularly important seasons in New England, and many of the plants that do well in this

climate are at their best in May or September. Within the garden we have set aside spaces designed to be at their peak at those times of the year, while the hot months of July and August provide a relatively quiet time, when the dominant colour is green and the full beauty of the surrounding trees can be appreciated.

One difficulty we encountered was the choice of appropriate hedging throughout the garden. Yew will grow happily in New England, but deer eat it, and here the deer population has exploded to almost plague-like proportions. Hornbeam or beech, our preferred deciduous alternatives, are naked for many months of the year in this climate. In the end, we opted for a compromise: the main approaches to the house have evergreen

hedges of holly (*Ilex* x *meserveae* 'China Girl'), and we have used hornbeam (*Carpinus betulus*) in the rest of the garden.

Late in the day we were asked to add a swimming pool to the design. The formality of our plan, with its repetition of axes, squares and rectangles, enabled us to place the pool garden so that it looked as if it had always been part of the original master plan. A 1.2m (4ft) fence around a swimming pool is a legal requirement in the United States, and here we used the local picket fencing to create a series of enclosures and arbours to reduce the impact of the fence itself.

Less than two years on, the clients have a garden which gives them pleasure at all times of the year, and which sets the house comfortably into the surrounding landscape.

OPPOSITE *The newly planted Amelanchier and Dogwood Walk, on the swimming pool side of the main lawn. The tiny flowers of the multi-stemmed shad bush are one of the earliest signs of spring in New England, appearing in April as the last snows disappear. We were lucky to obtain dogwoods that had been trained into balanced forms.*

RIGHT *The Chinese dogwood (Cornus kousa) is particularly resistant to disease and was chosen for a prominent position flanking the main lawn because of its value in every season: June flowers followed by strawberry-like fruit, good autumn colour and elegant mottled grey bark.*

BELOW LEFT *Six Japanese lilac (Syringa reticulata) trained as trees frame views from the house to the wisteria arbour beyond the swimming pool. This, too, is a four-season plant with scented flowers, fruit, autumn colour and copper bark.*

BELOW RIGHT *The flowers of the tulip tree (Liriodendron tulipifera) are one of the glories of native eastern American woodland.*

ABOVE *The Sunken Flower Garden in early September: tender* Salvia 'Indigo Spires' *mingles with* Gaura lindheimeri, Verbena bonariensis *and* Salvia uliginosa. *Above the wall, the drooping white panicles of* Hydrangea paniculata grandiflora *will turn a soft rosy hue.*

LEFT *Michaelmas daisies are useful late-flowering perennials, with flowers ranging in colour from white through pink and blue to purple. In the Spring and Autumn Walk next to the Sunken Flower Garden,* Aster amellus 'Moerheim Gem' *and the smaller-flowered* A. lateriflorus, *with an elegant arching habit, glow in the autumn light.*

Pyrus salicifolia 'Pendula'

Clematis recta with Alliums

Pot

Argyranthemum frutescens

Pot

Clematis recta with Alliums

Argyranthemum frutescens

Pyrus salicifolia 'Pendula'

Salvia sclarea var turkestanica

Rosa 'Bonica'

Ilex crenata

Ilex crenata

Rosa 'Bonica'

Salvia sclarea var turkestanica

Buddleja alternifolia with stachys

Stachys byzantina

Stachys byzantina

Buddleja alternifolia with stachys

Pot

Pot

Baptisia australis

Baptisia australis

Aster ericoides

Iris sibirica 'Caesar's Brother'

Rosa 'Alba Maxima'

Lysimachia clethroides

Polemonium Caeruleum

Polemonium caeruleum

Lysimachia Clethroides

Thalictrum flavum glaucum

Thalictrum flavum glaucum

Kalimeris mongolica

Calamintha nepeta nepeta

Calamintha nepeta nepeta

Kalimeris mongolica

Aster ericoides

Malus 'Snowdrift'

Malus 'Snowdrift'

Alchemilla mollis

Gaura lindheimeri

Gaura lindheimeri

Rosa 'Frances E. Lester'

Hydrangea paniculata 'Grandiflora'

Nepeta 'Six Hills Giant'

Salvia 'Indigo Spires'

Salvia 'Indigo Spires'

Nepeta 'Six Hills Giant'

Geranium sanguineum

Syringa persica

Lobelia Siphilitica

Lobelia Siphilitica

Ilex crenata

Ilex crenata

Veronicastrum virginicum

Veronicastrum virginicum

Physostegia virginiana 'Summer Snow'

Physostegia virginiana 'Summer Snow'

Argyranthemum frutescens

Box hedge

Box hedge

1m / 3ft

Pool

N ←

Seat

Viburnum x pragense

Aster 'Purple Dome'

Argyranthemum frutescens

Box hedge

Box hedge

Ilex crenata

Ilex crenata

Physostegia virginiana 'Summer Snow'

Physostegia virginiana 'Summer Snow'

Alchemilla Mollis

Nepeta 'Six Hills Giant'

Lobelia Siphilitica

Veronicastrum virginicum

Veronicastrum virginicum

Lobelia Siphilitica

Nepeta 'Six Hills Giant'

Geranium sanguineum

Syringa x persica

Hydrangea paniculata 'Grandiflora'

Salvia 'Indigo Spires'

Gaura lindheimeri

Gaura lindheimeri

Salvia 'Indigo Spires'

Rosa Ispahan

Rosa 'Thérèse Bugnet'

Aster ericoides

Malus 'Snowdrift'

Kalimeris Mongolica

Calamintha nepeta nepeta

Calamintha nepeta nepeta

Kalimeris mongolica

Malus 'Snowdrift'

Thalictrum flavum glaucum

Aster ericoides

Baptisia australis

Lysimachia clethroides

Polemonium caeruleum

Polemonium caeruleum

Lysimachia clethroides

Baptisia australis

Eleagnus umbellata

Geranium Sanguineum

Eleagnus umbellata

Pot

Stachys byzantina

Euphorbia myrsinites

Seat

Euphorbia myrsinites

Stachys byzantina

Pot

Pyrus Salicifolia 'Pendula'

Cephalaria gigantea

Ilex glabra

Salvia sclarea var turkestanica

Rosa 'Sir Thomas Lipton'

Ilex crenata

Ilex crenata

Rosa 'Sir Thomas Lipton'

Clematis recta

Ilex glabra

Salvia sclarea var turkestanica

Pyrus salicifolia 'Pendula'

Lespedeza thunbergii

Urn

Lespedeza thunbergii

Cephalaria gigantea

Viburnum plicatum 'Shasta'

Hornbeam hedge

A New Garden for a Restored Villa

We have been fortunate, over the years, to collaborate with the distinguished interior designer Jean Munro on a number of different projects. In 1994 she introduced us to Count Vittorio Marzotto and his wife, Simona, with whom she was working on the restoration of a villa in northern Italy. We were delighted to have the opportunity to work with them on the garden. The villa gardens of the Italian Renaissance have had a profound influence on the evolution of garden design, and to make a garden in Italy had long been something of a dream.

The Marzottos live in a little village in the Friuli region of north-east Italy, some 40 km (25 miles) from the Austrian Alps. The area was devastated by an earthquake in 1976, when many towns and villages had been reduced to rubble. Most of the rebuilding in the region consists of hastily erected unattractive modern houses made of cheap materials. However, Simona Marzotto has a business that restores houses, and she and her husband had gone to great lengths to use traditional materials as accurately as possible in the restoration of their own house.

When we first saw the site in the autumn of 1994, there was just building rubble and tatty grass around the house – a clean slate on which to work. All too often, our work is compromised or curtailed by having to reckon with existing structures or garden elements. Here we could design without encumbrance. This was a rare treat.

The Marzottos had a clear idea about the kind of garden they thought appropriate for the house. It should have historical associations – echoes of gardens past – but we should be prepared to use modern plant cultivars and up-to-date technology; this was not to be a fossil. Simona Marzotto has a passionate love of flowers and a serious interest in the medicinal properties of herbs and vegetables. A large cutting and vegetable garden was high on the priority list.

On our first visit we sketched out a rough plan. The fruit, vegetable and cutting garden would be laid out as an ornamental potager on the north side of the house, close to the kitchen, and the flower gardens would be at the front, facing south. The house was the dominant presence, and to complement it we decided to use evergreen oaks (*Quercus ilex*) grown as standards and then clipped into cubes. This would give us blocks of green some 3-4m (10-14ft) in the air, which would help to balance the proportions of the house and screen an ugly neighbouring barn.

On either side of the front door we placed box parterres, and beyond these a square lawn with flower beds in each corner. The proportions of the spaces that we were making were dictated by the house: hedges followed walls; paths were aligned on windows and doors. The key was to create

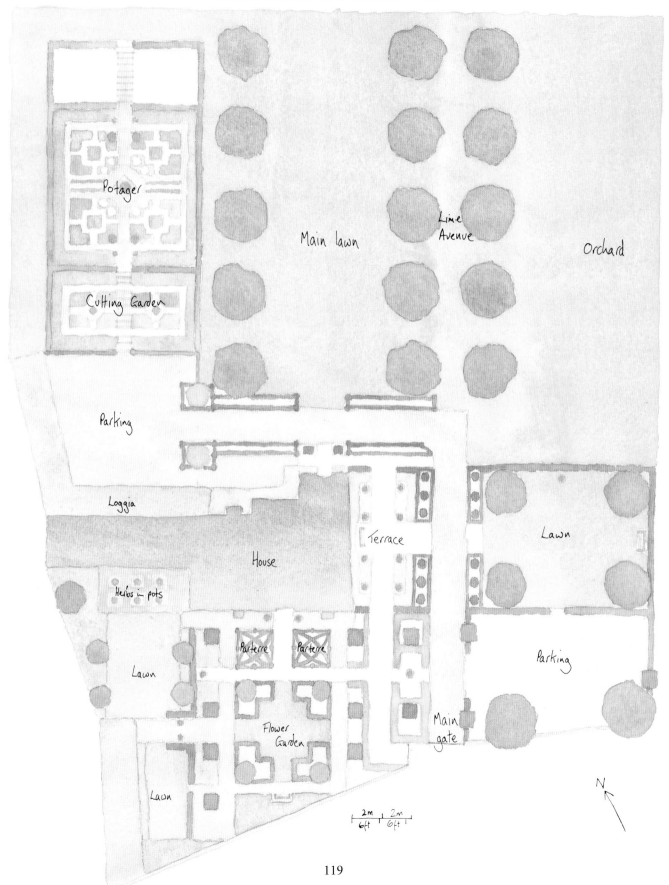

Potager

Cutting Garden

Main lawn

Lime
Avenue

Orchard

Parking

Loggia

Terrace

Lawn

House

Herbs in pots

Parterre   Parterre

Parking

Lawn

Main
gate

Flower
Garden

Lawn

2m
6ft

2m
6ft

N

ABOVE *A view from the loggia at the back of the house across the main lawn through the triple avenue of limes. Groups of terracotta pots, from the hills south of Florence, are planted and maintained by Nicholas Lambourne.*

variety within a harmonious whole. At the rear of the house, a loggia provided welcome shade from the summer sun. Here there would be low box-edged beds allowing views across the garden through a triple avenue of lime trees, to a hilltop town some 10 km (6 miles) away.

At this point we began to consider the hard surfaces we were to use. Simona Marzotto took us to look at what remained of the traditional building styles in the area, and we opted for a pale grey-brown limestone and large grey cobblestones. Simona also used her contacts to locate old stone slabs, and then embarked on the

Herculean task of measuring and numbering each slab as it arrived. Large drawings of the paths were prepared, and Simona, working to scale, positioned her numbered stones accordingly. This was a laborious task, but enabled us to avoid cutting or wasting stone, and also made laying the slabs much quicker.

The cobbles were laid on a sand and cement base, and then a dry mixture of sand and cement was brushed between them, covering about two thirds of each stone. For surfaces where we wanted a more informal feeling, we were able to use old terracotta brick. We were fortunate to have clients who not only understood the importance of

ABOVE *The flower gardens at the front of the house are defined by stone and cobble paths (a traditional local mixture), and box hedges kept at a height that suggests intimacy but allows views across the whole garden. Exuberant planting spills over and softens the hard edges, demonstrating the Italian influence softened with an English touch. Olive trees (Olea europea), brought in as large specimens, provide an instant maturity and act as anchors to the scheme. In gardens with as much detail as this one, expanses of grass can provide welcome relief, as well as holding the composition together.*

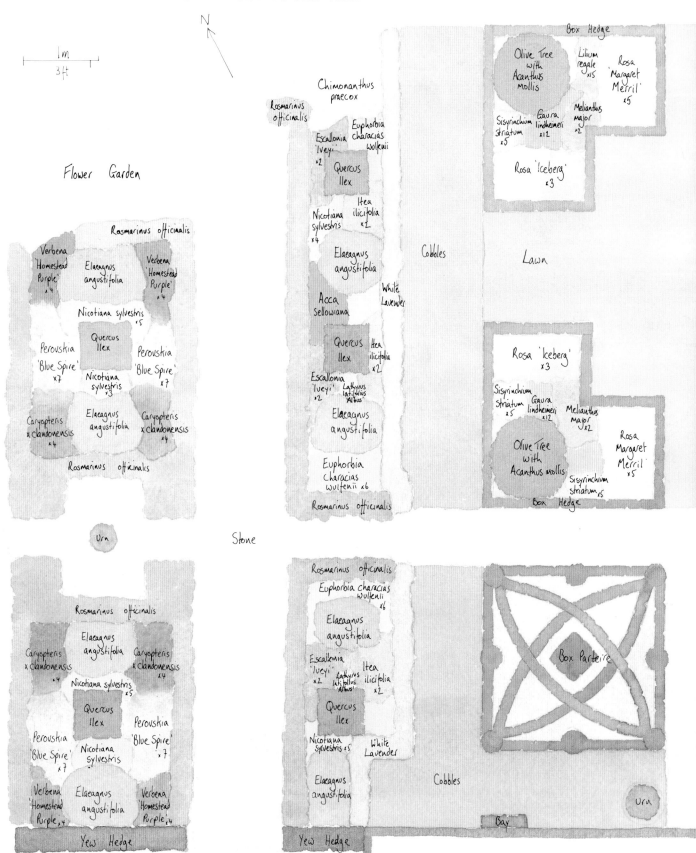

N

1 m
3 ft

Flower Garden

Top-left bed:

Rosmarinus officinalis

Verbena 'Homestead Purple' x4 · Elaeagnus angustifolia · Verbena 'Homestead Purple' x4

Nicotiana sylvestris x5

Perovskia 'Blue Spire' x7 · Quercus Ilex · Perovskia 'Blue Spire' x7

Nicotiana sylvestris x3

Caryopteris x clandonensis x4 · Elaeagnus angustifolia · Caryopteris x clandonensis x4

Rosmarinus officinalis

Urn

Bottom-left bed:

Rosmarinus officinalis

Caryopteris x clandonensis x4 · Elaeagnus angustifolia · Caryopteris x clandonensis x4

Nicotiana sylvestris x5

Perovskia 'Blue Spire' x7 · Quercus Ilex · Perovskia 'Blue Spire' x7

Nicotiana sylvestris

Verbena 'Homestead Purple' x4 · Elaeagnus angustifolia · Verbena 'Homestead Purple' x4

Yew Hedge

Stone

Top-right bed:

Rosmarinus officinalis

Chimonanthus praecox

Escallonia 'Iveyi' x2 · Euphorbia characias wulfenii

Quercus Ilex

Nicotiana sylvestris x4 · Itea ilicifolia x2

Elaeagnus angustifolia

Acca Sellowiana · White Lavender

Quercus Ilex · Itea ilicifolia x2

Escallonia 'Iveyi' x2 · Lathyrus latifolius 'Albus'

Elaeagnus angustifolia

Euphorbia characias wulfenii x6

Rosmarinus officinalis

Cobbles

Top-right box hedge bed:

Box Hedge

Olive Tree with Acanthus mollis · Lilium regale x15 · Rosa Margaret Merril x5

Sisyrinchium striatum x5 · Gaura lindheimeri x12 · Melianthus major x2

Rosa 'Iceberg' x3

Lawn

Mid-right box hedge bed:

Rosa 'Iceberg' x3

Sisyrinchium striatum x5 · Gaura lindheimeri x12 · Melianthus major x2

Olive Tree with Acanthus mollis · Sisyrinchium striatum x5 · Rosa Margaret Merril x5

Box Hedge

Bottom-right bed:

Rosmarinus officinalis

Euphorbia characias wulfenii x6

Elaeagnus angustifolia

Escallonia 'Iveyi' x2 · Lathyrus latifolius 'Albus' · Itea ilicifolia x2

Quercus Ilex

Nicotiana sylvestris x5 · White Lavender

Elaeagnus angustifolia

Yew Hedge · Bay

Cobbles

Box Parterre

Urn

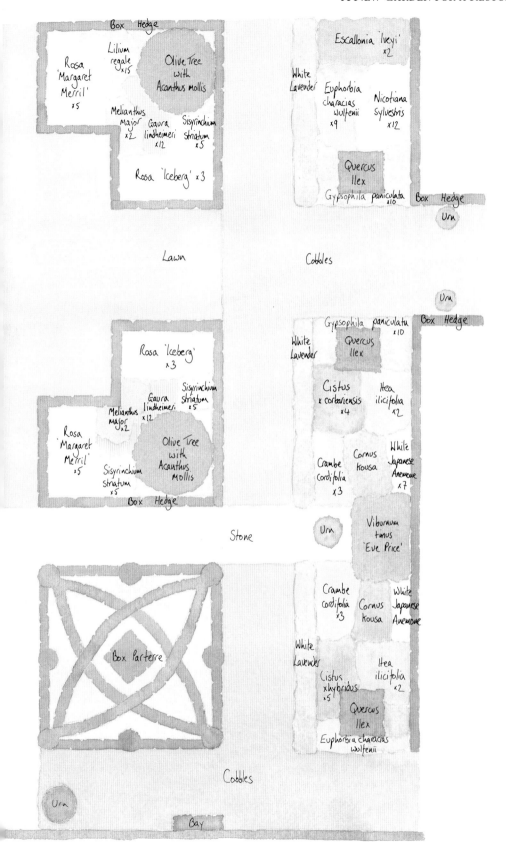

Box Hedge

Rosa
'Margaret
Merril'
x5

Lilium
regale
x15

Olive Tree
with
Acanthus mollis

Melianthus
Major
x2

Gaura
lindheimeri
x12

Sisyrinchium
striatum
x5

Rosa 'Iceberg' x3

Lawn

Escallonia 'Iveyi'
x2

White
Lavender

Euphorbia
characias
wulfenii
x9

Nicotiana
sylvestris
x12

Quercus
Ilex

Gypsophila paniculata
x10

Box Hedge

Urn

Cobbles

Urn

Rosa 'Iceberg'
x3

Gaura
lindheimeri
x12

Sisyrinchium
striatum
x5

Melianthus
Major
x2

Rosa
Margaret
Merril'
x5

Sisyrinchium
striatum
x5

Olive Tree
with
Acanthus
Mollis

Box Hedge

Gypsophila paniculata
x10

White
Lavender

Quercus
Ilex

Cistus
x corbariensis
x4

Itea
ilicifolia
x2

Crambe
cordifolia
x3

Cornus
kousa

White
Japanese
Anemone
x7

Stone

Urn

Viburnum
tinus
'Eve Price'

Crambe
cordifolia
x3

Cornus
kousa

White
Japanese
Anemone

Box Parterre

White
Lavender

Cistus
x hybridus
x5

Itea
ilicifolia
x2

Quercus
Ilex

Euphorbia characias
wulfenii

Cobbles

Urn

Bay

finding the right materials, but enjoyed the whole process of construction.

The nursery trade in Italy is justifiably famous for the size of its specimen plants. The Marzottos wanted the garden to look mature as quickly as possible, and with the help of Margheriti's nursery we were able to use yew that was already 1.8m (6ft) high, box the size we required, and specimen trees with an instant presence. Handling large plants is difficult and exhausting work, and the men from Margheriti's were fascinating to watch.

By the autumn of 1995 we had completed the master plan, laid out the hard surfaces, and planted the main structural elements. We then had to attend to the detail. At this point we were lucky to recruit, as Head Gardener, Nicholas Lambourne who had been working in the south of France. With his technical expertise (combined with a love of plants and an artist's eye), we could embark on the next phase of the project – planting flowers, herbs and vegetables – with confidence.

We began to fill the flower beds we had created while the sun was still warm and the plants had a chance to establish before winter closed in. The temperatures in this region vary greatly, from hot (up to 35°C (95°F)) and dry in summer, to as cold as -10°C (14°F) and wet in winter. Fortunately, the soil is free-draining so plants do not sit with their roots in cold water. Casualties from the first planting were few, and in spring 1996 we were able to complete the task, mostly with plants from England, brought to Italy by lorry. We found that this was the only way to get the broad range of material we needed.

Thanks to the hot Italian sun and effective automatic irrigation, the growth in the garden during its first full season has been prolific. It is sometimes hard to remember that less than two years before, this fine old house sat in a bare field.

ABOVE Angelica gigas

A Selection From The Potager

Herbs

Hyssop	Angelica
Tarragon	Basil
Borage	Thyme
Lemon Verbena	Chives

Italian and English Parsley
Narrow and Broad Leaf Sage

Soft Fruit

Rhubarb ('Victoria' + 'Temperley Early')
Blackcurrant ('Ben Lomond' + 'Seabrook's Black')
Whitecurrant ('White Versailles')
Gooseberry ('Whinham's Industry')
Raspberry ('Autumn Joy' + 'Glen May')

Roses For Cutting

'Polar Star'	'Gertrude Jekyll'
'Margaret Merril'	'Graham Thomas'
'Winchester Cathedral'	'Othello'

N

1m
3ft

PREVIOUS PAGES *At the heart of the potager a standard bay (Laurus nobilis) acts as a counterpoint to eight standard 'Iceberg' roses. The sphere of bay is complemented by metal arches used as frames for runner beans. The beans hang down inside the frame and are easy to harvest.*

BELOW *Grown formally in clearly divided compartments with a strong ground plan of cobble and brick paths, the beauty of vegetables can be enjoyed to the full. Metal arches and hedges of box and hornbeam hold the design together during the winter months, when the beds in the potager are* virtually empty. *Here, in summer, tomatoes are interspersed with leeks and underplanted with a froth of carrots. The outrageous blood-red stems and deeply veined leaves of ruby chard will remain long into the winter, providing fresh fare for the household.*

A GARDEN FOR SCULPTURE

ABOVE *The White Garden is enclosed on two sides by mature yew hedges that make a perfect backdrop for garden ornaments. To the east and north, espalier apples and the catalpa walk complete the walls of this 'room' which is further defined by the 'floor' made of rectangles of red brick infilled with fine gravel.*

Restoring the walled gardens at Dunsborough Park in Surrey is a large and challenging undertaking. Plans now exist for nearly the whole complex of gardens and the planting of the walled area to the north east of the house, shown in the plan, has been implemented (although still very immature). The main mixed borders, now in their second year, already look good, with a rhythm established by standard wisterias and viburnums.

Parts of Dunsborough Park date to the fifteenth century but the wings and central portion visible today are seventeenth- and eighteenth-century respectively. The house has also had several alterations and additions over the last hundred years. A complex of attractive glasshouses was constructed in the mid nineteenth century and the walled gardens were almost certainly built around this time, although some of the walls may well be earlier. During the 1939-45 war, Sir Oliver Simmonds made a fortune inventing and patenting nylon locking nuts, which allowed him to add some interesting areas to the Victorian garden, including an elaborate secret water garden as well as a rock garden and rustic swimming pool. More recent owners have made less fortunate additions.

When the gardens were acquired by Baron and Baroness Sweerts de Landas Wyborgh in 1994, the basic pattern of brick walls and old yew hedges remained, providing the garden

with strong structural elements that needed little modification. But the garden was a sad relic of departed glory. No new constructive planting in beds or borders had taken place for many years. There are still areas to be tackled but a large restoration project benefits from a slow approach, allowing further ideas to develop as sections are completed.

Dolf Sweerts is a dealer in antique garden ornaments, and although his main 'For Sale' corner is in the courtyard, we have designed places in many of the areas of the walled garden where urns and statues on plinths can be displayed. Dolf's business means that the garden is always on show to potential customers, and the ornaments, although often temporary, give a distinguished air.

The Sweerts wanted to keep the central space available for a marquee. This area is aligned on the main glasshouse entrance and on the gates in the far wall to the north. We retained some of the original architectural planting here, including hedges and the four golden-leaved Irish yews, planted as a square, which make a strong statement by the glasshouse, from where they frame the gates on the other side of the garden. Old espalier apples, 3m (10ft) tall and with four horizontals, made an avenue on either side of the central area of grass. Unfortunately, although a wonderful feature, not all the apples were in good condition, but after

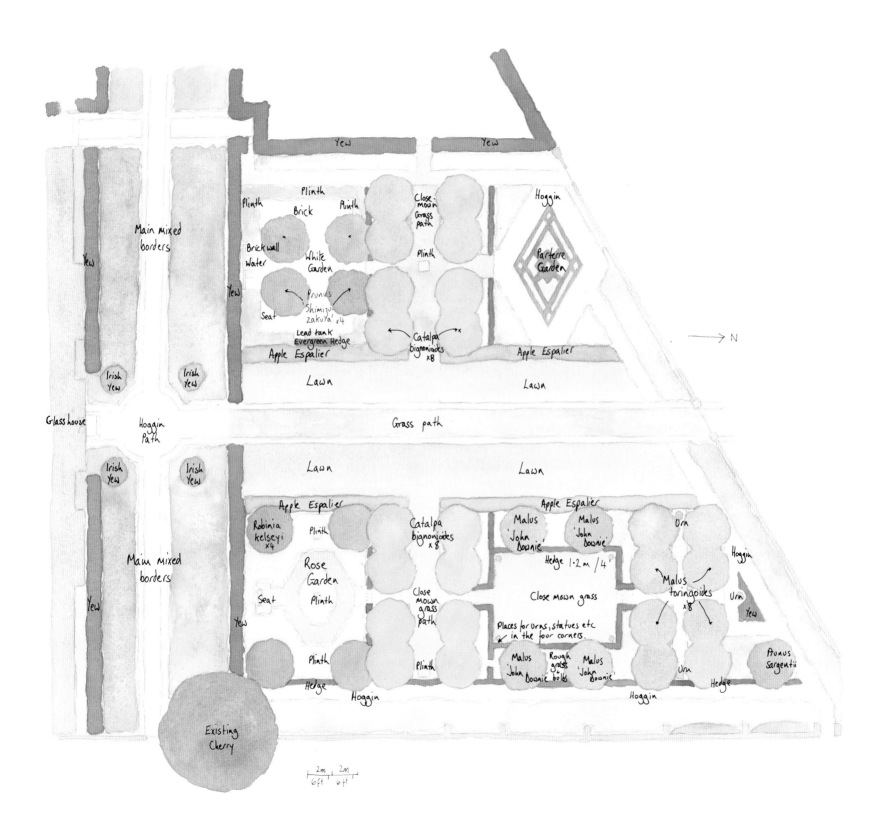

Main mixed borders

Yew

Yew

Yew

Irish Yew

Irish Yew

Irish Yew

Irish Yew

Glass house

Hoggin Path

Main mixed borders

Existing Cherry

Yew

Yew

Yew

Yew

Plinth

Plinth

Plinth

Plinth

Brick

White Garden

Brick wall Water

Seat

Lead tank Evergreen Hedge

Apple Espalier

Close mown Grass path

Plinth

Prunus 'Shimizu-zakura' x4

Catalpa bignonioides x8

Hoggin

Parterre Garden

Apple Espalier

Lawn

Lawn

Grass path

Lawn

Lawn

Apple Espalier

Apple Espalier

Robinia kelseyi x4

Plinth

Rose Garden

Plinth

Seat

Plinth

Plinth

Hedge

Hoggin

Catalpa bignonioides x8

Close mown grass path

Plinth

Malus 'John Downie'

Malus 'John Downie'

Urn

Hedge 1.2 m / 4'

Close mown grass

Places for urns, statues etc in the four corners.

Malus 'John Downie'

Rough grass + bulbs

Malus 'John Downie'

Hoggin

Malus toringoides x8

Urn

Urn

Urn

Yew

Hoggin

Prunus sargentii

Hedge

→ N

2m / 6ft   2m / 6ft

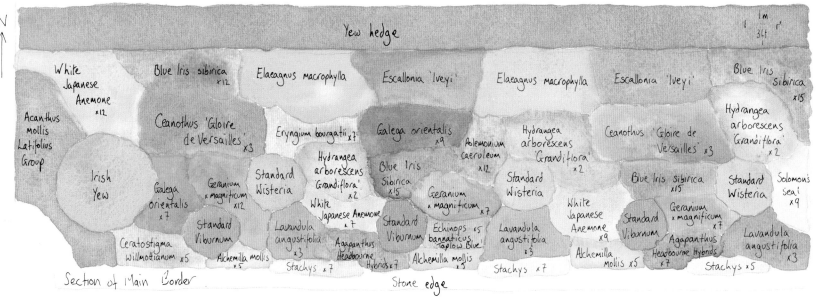

Section of Main Border

RIGHT *The main mixed borders, looking west towards the house. Architectural wisterias and viburnums, grown in a formal rhythm, hold together the design of looser flowers and silvery foliage plants.*

LEFT *The dark yew hedge provides a dramatic background to echinops,* Galega orientalis, *globe headed alliums (*Allium christophii*) and English lavender, with silver-leaved* Stachys byzantina *at the front. Lilies and self-seeded opium poppies are left over from the first season.*

much consideration we decided to retain them for as long as possible. The plans for the rest of this walled section had to 'work' around these fixtures which left plenty of space for dividing the area into a series of smaller gardens.

We defined the wide central lawn by using paving slabs to make a narrower grass walk. This linked the space with the glasshouse and golden yews, and with the main mixed borders where paving slabs are also used as edging. A central cross alley of Indian bean tree (*Catalpa bignonioides*) which flowers in summer, running east-west, is perhaps the most imposing, from an architectural point of view. It completes the division of the whole area into four, in which we have made

a series of quite definite enclosures. These are marked out by verticals – small broad-headed trees with an almost domestic connotation (robinias, cherries, crabs and the catalpas) rather than by continuous hedging. The Rose Garden is to have four corner trees: fragrant pink-flowered *Robinia kelseyi*. The White Garden is dominated by four *Prunus* 'Shimizu-zakura' – also planted in the corners – one of the loveliest of the white Japanese cherries, with drooping long-stalked flower clusters. In the north-east corner, six crabs (*Malus toringoides*) with grey deeply divided leaves and white flowers in May, followed by autumn fruits, make a symmetrical alley next to a square of 'John Downie' crabs – excellent for crab apple jelly.

Hidden among the vertical trees is a square of close-mown grass, hedged with yews, that can be used to display garden ornaments or sculptures. A small Parterre Garden in the north-west corner is planned to feature a central diamond-shaped pool but will be planted until the children are older, with corner beds of deep purple flowers and bronze and purple foliage plants.

The layout of the double borders stretching east-west on either side of the Irish yews is basically unaltered but we have widened the path to make it broad enough for two people to walk abreast and edged the beds with stone slabs to match those that define the central grass walk. We have completely replanted these borders in a less

cottagey style than many of our designs, as Dolf Sweerts' classic ornaments, found throughout the garden, seemed to call for a tailored approach. Standard wisterias towards the back and viburnums at the front establish a rhythm along their length. Repeated blocks of blue, mauve and white flowers, mixed with some grey foliage plants, blend with the rather dominant golden yews which remain a centrepiece where the path broadens into a circle. Lady's mantle and grey-leaved stachys spill over the stone edging and complete the repetition of colour and texture at ground level. Now in their second year, the borders have filled out, and are well maintained by the Sweerts' gardener and his assistant.

131

An Elegant Villa Garden

Indian bean trees, Catalpa bignonioides, *flank the terrace. With large leaves and foxglove-like flowers* (ABOVE) *borne in panicles in July and August, the white petals marked with yellow and purple, these trees are grand enough to complement the house. The 'beans'* (BELOW), *most visible in autumn as the leaves fall, are almost as decorative as the flowers.*

We have been lucky to have made more than one garden for Jil Sander (see page 100). Recently she acquired two neighbouring houses in Hamburg, imposing eighteenth-century villas, the grounds of which had once stretched south to the Outer Alster lake. Today a public park and a busy road cuts off the gardens about 100 metres (yards) below the houses. One villa was to be Jil's own town house, the other to be adapted as the head-quarters of her fashion business.

The bulk of our work concerned her new home. The garden, reached by steep stone steps, lies below the house and, as we found it, sloped gently towards a mature weeping beech which effectively occupied the last quarter of the garden space. Jil wanted something elegant and simple in outline, not too flowery (the flowers are at Plön) and enough new planting to ensure privacy and security. At the same time it was important to keep the traditional view of the houses for those boating on the lake although this conflicted with the need for privacy. There had to be compromises but sometimes when limits are imposed from outside the work flourishes.

Today the completed garden respects the city and its landscape but allows Jil an almost secret oasis. Tall beech hedges, chosen for their tawny golden leaves in winter, enclose the garden. Rhododendrons, the beautiful

'Cunningham's White', with pink tinged buds opening to purest snow, and banks of knee-high box keep the garden green in winter. We designed a generous terrace, in keeping with the scale of the house, which demanded a wide base to support it. Below, down more steps, the ground was levelled as far as the beech and, now, narrow alleys of globe-headed trees reinforce the outer hedge, lining axial gravelled paths, while pyramids of free-standing yew flank a central panel of grass. It is an austere design but seems to satisfy 'the genius of the place', which a more elaborate layout might have destroyed. It also suits Jil's city *persona* and, for us, was a chance to pay tribute to her own fashion work, celebrated for its simplicity and minimalism.

On the terrace there was space for four trees and beds, planted with massed box. Pots will be filled with plants with softer shapes to give summer interest. Two troughs, below the balustrades, catch water gurgling from masks, disguising and deadening traffic and city noises. Three sets of steps lead to the newly levelled area below, where the alleys

Elevation showing steps, water spouts and balustrade.

and yews give vertical interest and a third dimension to the garden. Gravel paths curve round, reflecting the shape of the south side of the house, and meet at the bottom of the level garden, where we plan to place a stone seat. It was originally intended to back the seat with dark yew but the city wished to keep a more open view.

Hamburg winters are cold so plants have to be tough. Few of the broad-leaved evergreens we use in gardens nearer home will survive the low temperatures, when the lake freezes for skating and there are elaborate fairs, reminiscent of seventeenth-century England and paintings by Brueghel. We went with Jil to Bruns Nursery near the border with Holland, with clear ideas as to the type of plants needed but without a fixed list. This is an exciting way to work and enabled the whole team – client, designers, contractor and nurseryman – to be involved. For the upper terrace, Indian bean trees (*Catalpa bignonioides*), grand enough to complement the house, were chosen. For the alleys we found standard *Prunus fruticosa* 'Globosa', with dense twiggy heads and shining leaves in summer.

The garden is not a big one and its transformation required careful planning. Richard Patrick came from Plön to help supervise. By the autumn of 1996 the garden was complete. It is always an exciting and nervous moment when designs are realized. We feel happy with the results and hope that for Jil Sander the garden will be a lasting and peaceful haven.

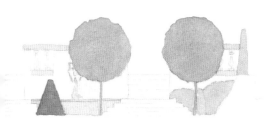

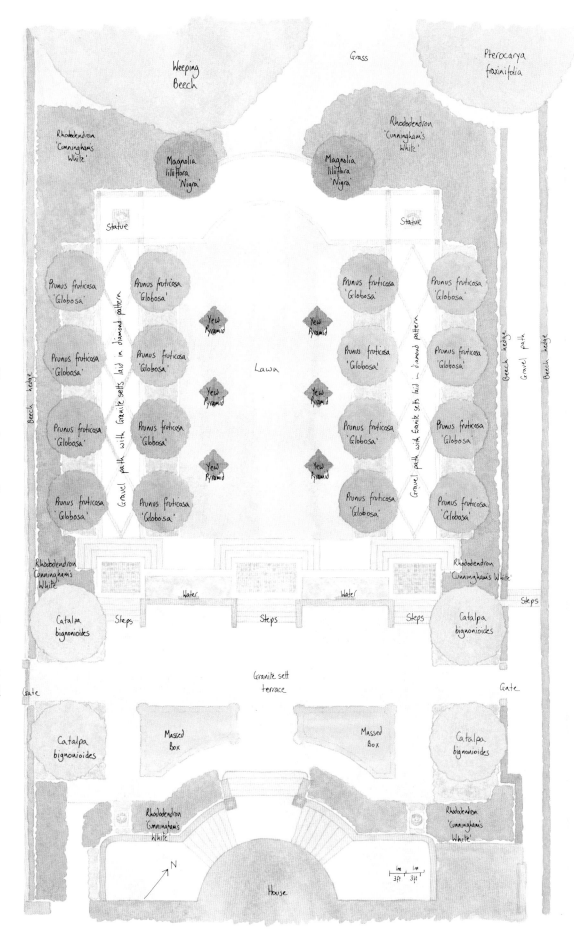

A Secret Urban Garden

Stephen and Julie Riley live in a terraced house in south-west London. When we were asked to help them with the garden, they had just finished renovating the interior of the house and Julie was expecting her first baby. They already had lots of ideas as to what they wanted, but had been unable to put together a plan that would fulfil their hopes and their requirements. They had decided to ask our advice because they realised they wanted a professionally designed garden.

Most importantly, they wanted a lawn for the baby to play on, and a terrace for use as an outdoor dining-room. They would need a garden shed big enough to house the mower and garden furniture, and Stephen suggested that a piece of architectural whimsy might be fun. Julie also wanted somewhere to grow vegetables and have flowers for cutting, and Stephen had a hankering for a parterre.

The garden is a rectangle, 14m (47ft) long by 5.5m (18ft) wide, with brick walls on three sides and the house on the fourth. The walls are only 1.5m (5ft) high, and since the custom in the nineteenth century was for building apprentices to practise their bricklaying skills on garden walls, they are uneven in construction and uncertain in appearance. The only other component to consider was a white-flowering cherry tree.

Neither Stephen nor Julie were gardeners, so they were happy to leave specific plant selections to us, but they did have clear ideas about the planting. They wanted it to be quite formal, and the effects kept broad and strong. Height could be achieved by means of archways or trelliswork clad with scented climbers. The rear of the house had been reorganized so that two pairs of big french

RIGHT *The view down the garden which, towards the end of its first summer, is starting to mature. The colours of the slate mosaic are echoed in the mainly silver-grey with pale azure blue planting.*

ABOVE LEFT *Looking back towards the house, Japanese anemone 'Honorine Jobert', perennial forget-me-nots (Brunnera macrophylla), stinking hellebores (Helleborus foetidus) and Alexandria laurel (Danae racemosa) are planted beneath the cherry tree.*

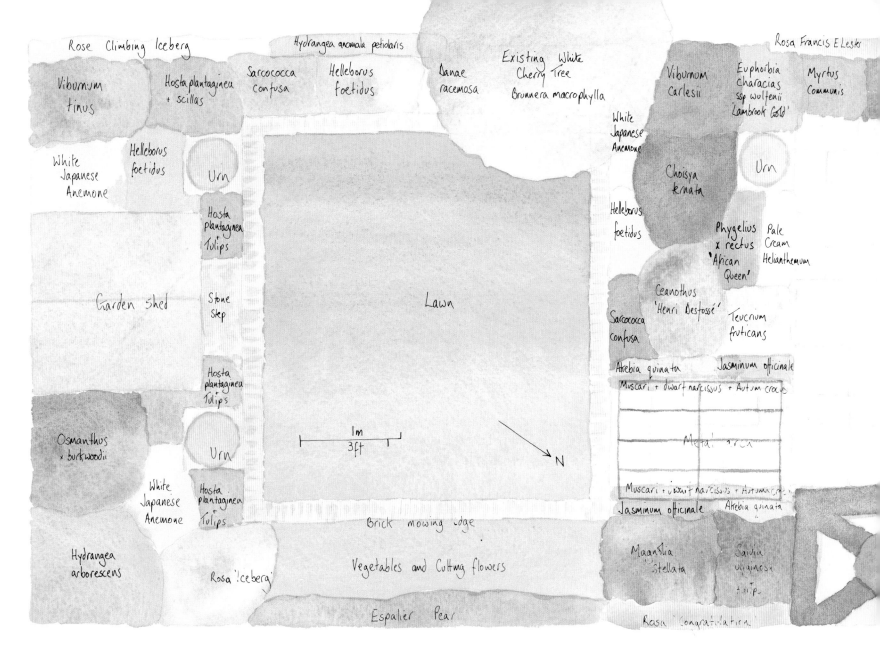

Rose Climbing Iceberg

Hydrangea anomala petiolaris

Rosa Francis E Lester

Viburnum tinus

Hosta plantaginea + scillas

Sarcococca confusa

Helleborus foetidus

Danae racemosa

Existing White Cherry Tree

Brunnera macrophylla

Viburnum Carlesii

Euphorbia Characias ssp wulfenii 'Lambrook Gold'

Myrtus Communis

White Japanese Anemone

Helleborus foetidus

White Japanese Anemone

Choisya ternata

Urn

Urn

Helleborus foetidus

Phygelius x rectus 'African Queen'

Pale Cream Helianthemum

Hosta plantaginea Tulips

Garden Shed

Stone Step

Lawn

Ceanothus 'Henri Desfossé'

Sarcococca confusa

Teucrium fruticans

Akebia quinata

Jasminum officinale

Muscari + dwarf narcissus + Autumn crocus

Hosta plantaginea + Tulips

1m
3ft

N

Metal arch

Osmanthus x burkwoodii

Urn

Muscari + dwarf narcissus + Autumn cr...

White Japanese Anemone

Hosta plantaginea + Tulips

Jasminum officinale

Akebia quinata

Brick mowing edge

Hydrangea arborescens

Rosa 'Iceberg'

Vegetables and Cutting flowers

Magnolia Stellata

Salvia uliginosa + tulip

Espalier Pear

Rosa 'Congratulation'

windows opened directly into the garden, and they asked if the planting could be architectural enough to sustain this view throughout the year. As a final point, they wanted a colour scheme of blues, whites and creams, with a little pale pink.

Designing for such a confined space, with so many specific requests and a limited budget, can be both a blessing and a curse. It is a pleasure to have clients who know what they want, but making the whole work can be tricky. We decided to divide the garden

roughly into three, with a flagstone terrace occupying the central space. This would be reached by means of two smaller stone terraces leading directly from the french windows, and a single path would lead into the final section of the garden – the lawn.

Metal arches, made for us in Somerset, frame both entrances to the main terrace, and a third makes a tunnel at the exit. This enhances the idea of the space as a room, with doors in and out of it. We also introduced the sound of water with a trough

and a spout, set against the wall.

The one thing we could not find room for was Stephen's parterre; we were able to introduce some formality into the planting with a patterned box hedge and clipped standard bay on one side of the terrace, but a proper parterre seemed impossible. We suggested instead a mosaic of cut slate, in blue and green with a little red, as the central feature of the terrace. The garden walls have been given a colour wash to tie in the different colours of brick, and a simple run

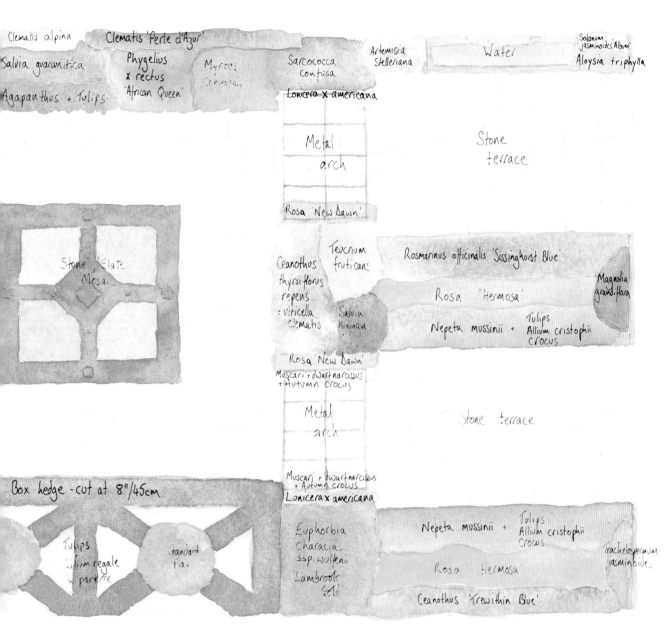

Clematis alpina

Clematis 'Perle d'Azur'

Salvia guaranitica

Phygelius x rectus 'African Queen'

Myrtus communis

Sarcococca confusa

Artemisia Stelleriana

Water

Solanum jasminoides Album'

Aloysia triphylla

Agapanthus + Tulips

Lonicera x americana

Metal arch

Stone terrace

Rosa 'New Dawn'

Stone Slate Mosaic

Ceanothus thyrsiflorus repens + Viticella clematis

Teucrium fruticans

Salvia oliviana

Rosmarinus officinalis 'Sissinghurst Blue'

Rosa 'Hermosa'

Nepeta mussinii + Tulips Allium cristophii crocus

Magnolia grandiflora

Rosa New Dawn

Muscari + dwarf narcissus + Autumn crocus

Metal arch

Stone terrace

Muscari + dwarf narcissus + Autumn crocus

Lonicera x americana

Box hedge - cut at 8"/45cm

Tulips Lilium regale in parterre

standard bay

Euphorbia Characias ssp. wulfenii 'Lambrook Gold'

Nepeta mussinii + Tulips Allium cristophii crocus

Rosa Hermosa

Ceanothus 'Trewithin Blue'

Trachelospermum jasminoides

of trellis panels on top provides sufficient height for both privacy and climbers. At the far end of the garden, the shed is placed centrally and painted in a gothic fashion, with colours chosen to tie in with the walls and the slate mosaic on the terrace.

The garden was completed in the autumn of 1995, and in its first full season climbers are starting to cover walls, arches and trelliswork. Stephen and Julie, with their son Hector, have a garden that is a central part of their lives – a source of pride and pleasure.

TOP RIGHT *The water trough full of cobbles is safe for children. It was made by simply standing up some stone slabs left over from making the terraces, binding them with an iron strap and then sealing the interior with fibreglass. Fast-growing Solanum jasminoides 'Album', the white potato flower, will cover this wall within a year.*

RIGHT *The simple box pattern anchors one side of the terrace planting. The compartments allow for a variety of planting, one year white tulips followed by Regal lilies, the next year something bolder.*

137

OPPOSITE *A view down one of the diagonal paths in the Cutting Garden.*

BELOW *In the Antechamber the borders are given direction by symmetrically placed small trees. The Luna pot, framed by hydrangeas, makes a focal point in front of the privet hedge. Shallow grass steps, edged with stone, are lined with native sweet pepper bush (Clethra alnifolia), and dark shiny leaved inkberry (Ilex glabra).*

A WOODLAND CUTTING GARDEN

Alex and Gabrielle Sheshunoff live in Austin, Texas, but spend their summers at Prout's Neck, on the rocky Atlantic shore of Maine. In 1994 they acquired just over 3 acres (1 ha) of native woodland, across the road from their house and only a hundred yards from the shore. The Sheshunoffs already owned a Garden House next to the new land – which had been scheduled for building. To keep this area as woodland and garden would benefit the whole community.

In August 1994 the Sheshunoffs asked me to visit and discuss the future of this piece of woodland. It consisted of a major breeding ground for mosquitoes to the north; an area of exposed rock ledge in the centre; and deeper soil to the south. At the time, they envisaged keeping it natural – just removing dead trees and branches, and cutting enough undergrowth to allow winding paths through the wood. Moss could be encouraged in the shadiest areas, and raised wooden walkways at the northern end would allow access. The wood was mainly of native spruce (*Picea glauca*), birch (*Betula papyrifera*), ash (*Fraxinus americana*), white oaks (*Quercus alba*), wild cherry (*Prunus serotina*) and red maple (*Acer rubra*), with alder (*Alnus rugosa* (syn *A. serrulata*)) in the damper patches, all with an understorey of deciduous holly (*Ilex verticillata*), chokeberry (*Prunus virginiana*) and the alien multiflora rose, which seeds in wherever there is space, and dog's tooth violets (*Erythronium dens-canis*) as spring groundcover. There was nothing of outstanding beauty or botanical rarity.

We worked out a clearance programme for the winter and spring, and were to meet again on site in August the following year. By then, however, Gabrielle had become an enthusiastic flower arranger, and was using florists' flowers. We were going to need flowers for the house.

We visited two traditional cutting gardens on the island of Mount Desert further north, and decided to make a new enclosed cutting garden in the damp area to the north – which would need new topsoil. It was also decided to make the whole plot into more of a real garden, improving the woodland but making the rock ledge into a moss garden and creating a pool surrounded by multi-stemmed birch (*Betula lenta*) which would come as a surprise as you climb over the rock ridges.

The woodland remains naturalistic in feel, with the perimeter planting thickened, but we have made a series of linked open and closed gardens within, that allow the visitor to move from sunlight to shadow and back to open glades. Eventually, none of these garden areas will be visible from neighbouring houses or from the road.

The Cutting Garden has evolved as two parts. Almost square (approximately 22 x 22m/ 75 x 75ft), with beds and paths leading diagonally from a central path, it is now preceded by a formal Antechamber (10 x 22m/ 37 x 77ft) aligned on the existing Garden House, around which my American associate, Nan Sinton, had designed a cottage garden several years previously.

By spring 1996 most of the preparatory work had been done, and many of the schemes are realised, although the moss garden needs time to become established under dense spruce, and the forest pool garden is immature. Both the Cutting Garden and the formal Antechamber are

Salvia 'Van Houttei'

Salvia 'Purple Majesty'

Helianthus 'Italian White'

Lablab purpureus

Rudbeckia hirta

Dahlia 'Arabian Nights'

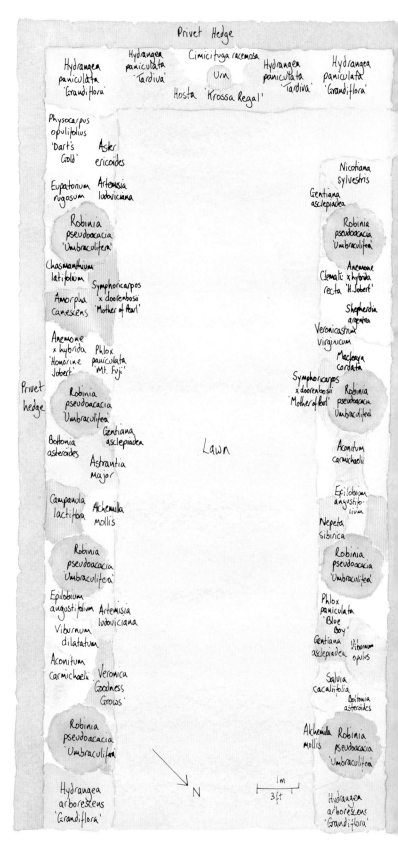

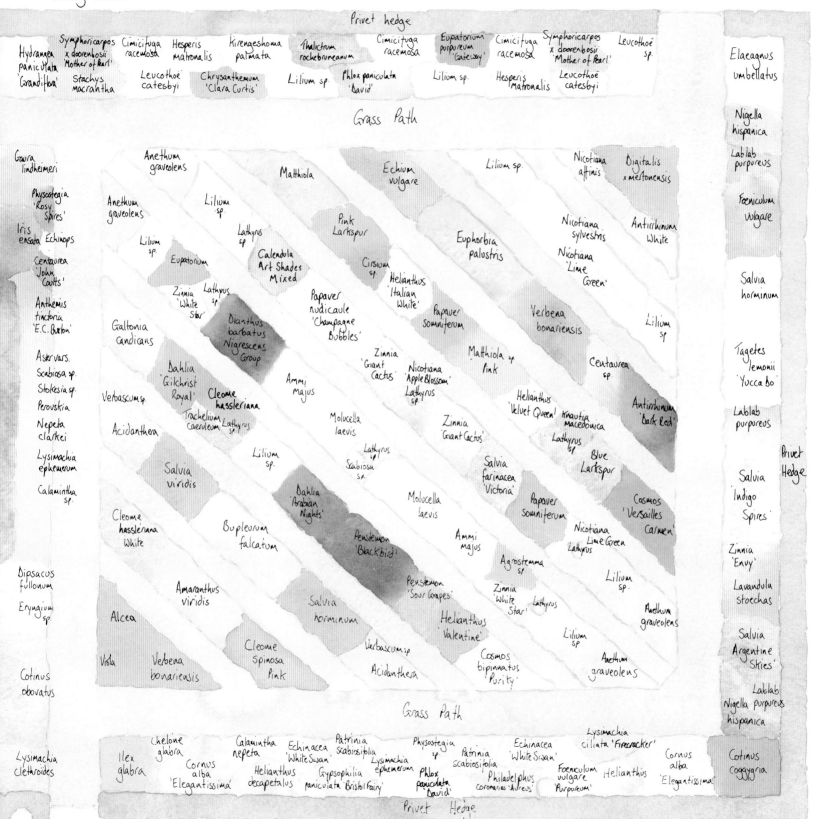

Cutting Garden

Privet hedge

Hydrangea paniculata 'Grandiflora' | Symphoricarpos x doorenbosii 'Mother of Pearl' | Cimicifuga racemosa | Hesperis matronalis | Kirengeshoma palmata | Thalictrum rochebruneanum | Cimicifuga racemosa | Eupatorium purpureum 'Gateway' | Cimicifuga racemosa | Symphoricarpos x doorenbosii 'Mother of Pearl' | Leucothoë sp.

Stachys macrantha | Leucothoë catesbyi | Chrysanthemum 'Clara Curtis' | Lilium sp. | Phlox paniculata 'David' | Lilium sp. | Hesperis matronalis | Leucothoë catesbyi

Elaeagnus umbellatus

Grass Path

Nigella hispanica

Gaura lindheimeri

Anethum graveolens

Matthiola

Echium vulgare

Lilium sp.

Nicotiana affinis | Digitalis x mertonensis

Lablab purpureus

Physostegia 'Rosy Spires'

Anethum graveolens

Lilium sp.

Pink Larkspur

Nicotiana sylvestris | Antirrhinum White

Foeniculum vulgare

Iris ensata | Echinops

Lilium sp.

Eupatorium

Lathyrus sp.

Calendula Art Shades Mixed

Cirsium sp.

Euphorbia palustris

Nicotiana 'Lime Green'

Salvia horminum

Centaurea 'John Coutts'

Zinnia 'White Star' | Lathyrus sp.

Helianthus 'Italian White'

Papaver somniferum

Lilium sp

Anthemis tinctoria 'E.C. Buxton'

Papaver nudicaule 'Champagne Bubbles'

Verbena bonariensis

Galtonia candicans

Dianthus barbatus Nigrescens Group

Zinnia 'Giant Cactus'

Matthiola 'Pink'

Centaurea sp.

Tagetes 'lemonii' Yucca bo

Aster vars. Scabiosa sp.

Dahlia 'Gilchrist Royal'

Ammi majus

Nicotiana 'Apple Blossom' | Lathyrus sp.

Antirrhinum 'Dark Red'

Stokesia sp.

Verbascum sp.

Cleome hassleriana

Helianthus 'Velvet Queen' | Knautia macedonica

Lablab purpureus

Perovskia

Acidanthera

Trachelium caeruleum | Lathyrus sp.

Molucella laevis

Zinnia 'Giant Cactus'

Lathyrus sp.

Nepeta clarkei

Lathyrus sp.

Blue Larkspur

Lysimachia ephemerum

Salvia viridis

Lilium sp.

Scabiosa sp.

Salvia farinacea 'Victoria'

Papaver somniferum

Cosmos 'Versailles Carmen'

Salvia Indigo Spires

Calamintha sp.

Cleome hassleriana White

Dahlia 'Arabian Nights'

Molucella laevis

Nicotiana Lime Green | Lathyrus

Bupleurum falcatum

Penstemon 'Blackbird'

Ammi majus

Zinnia 'Envy'

Dipsacus fullonum

Amaranthus viridis

Penstemon 'Sour Grapes'

Agrostemma sp.

Lilium sp.

Lavandula stoechas

Eryngium sp.

Alcea

Salvia horminum

Zinnia 'White Star' | Lathyrus

Anethum graveolens

Helianthus 'Valentine'

Lilium sp.

Salvia 'Argentine Skies'

Cotinus obovatus

Viola

Verbena bonariensis

Cleome spinosa Pink

Verbascum sp

Acidanthera

Cosmos bipinnatus 'Purity'

Anethum graveolens

Lablab Nigella purpureus hispanica

Grass Path

Lysimachia clethroides

Ilex glabra

Chelone glabra

Cornus alba 'Elegantissima'

Calamintha nepeta

Helianthus decapetalus

Echinacea 'White Swan'

Gypsophila paniculata 'Bristol Fairy'

Patrinia scabiosifolia

Lysimachia ephemerum

Physostegia sp.

Phlox paniculata 'David'

Patrinia scabiosifolia

Philadelphus coronarius 'Aureus'

Echinacea 'White Swan'

Lysimachia ciliata 'Firecracker'

Foeniculum vulgare 'Purpureum'

Helianthus

Cornus alba 'Elegantissima'

Cotinus coggyria

Privet Hedge

Privet Hedge

surrounded by a 1.5m (5ft) privet hedge. In the Antechamber, perennial borders, linked by a rhythm of globe locusts (*Robinia pseudoacacia* 'Umbraculifera'), frame the lawn. By August, architectural annuals such as the tall tobacco plant (*Nicotiana sylvestris*) and *Verbena bonariensis* are 2.5m (8ft) tall. Veronicas, phlox, asters and eupatoriums with hostas will soon bulk up the beds.

In the Cutting Garden trees had been removed to open up the whole area and to provide planting spaces. The unusual pattern of diagonal beds and paths in the central square, copied from a garden I had seen in Mount Desert, were constructed. The layout

ABOVE *In a clearing in the woods, the pool has been dug out and lined with butyl, grass has been sown and turf laid, and the multi-stemmed birch trees have been planted.*

LEFT *Looking across the Cutting Garden towards the Antechamber and Garden House. These two enclosed gardens are very structured, with globe locusts giving vertical strength, and the horizontal pattern of the diagonal beds a linear dimension.*

allows views across the rows of plants. Grass paths between each bed are 60cm (24in) wide and edged with cedar boards that will 'silver' over the years. The beds themselves are 1.2m (4ft) wide, and in them plants are massed in 1.2m sq (4ft sq) blocks, with some, such as tall nicotiana and cosmos, being given twice the space. Initially there were problems with soil compaction, but by the end of May beds with new topsoil were ready for planting. The borders around the diagonal beds had been planted with shrubs and perennials, with the climbing blue hyacinth bean, *Lablab purpureus*, decorating the bamboo tripods.

Plants were grown on by local nurserymen, many from seed obtained in England, to be ready for 30th May – well after the average date for the last frost. There were a few disappointments and some of the plants went in late, but by August, much of the Cutting Garden looked as planned.

Most of Gabrielle's flowers now come from the Cutting Garden, and soon she will be able to pick branches of foliage to add to her effects. The whole garden combines domesticity and naturalism with the circular forest pool providing a touch of drama.

A Mediterranean Scheme

TOP *The ornamental pool on the lawn outside the loggia reflects the imposing cork oak that overhangs it. An overflow from this pool splashes down into another where the water is filtered and recirculated.*

ABOVE *The main entrance, paved with cobblestones and terracotta tiles, is decorated with pots: seasonal combinations of plants by the door and large lemon trees, seen here waiting to be planted, for structure.*

I have visited many French and Italian Riviera gardens, as well as gardens in California, but it wasn't until the week of the Chelsea Flower Show in 1995, when we met a client with land by the Mediterranean, that we were asked to make a garden using tender and sub-tropical plants. The owner and her husband were just starting to build a new house in southern Spain, near one of the most beautiful golf courses in the world. She had read many of my books and liked the same sort of planting effects that I do. Her husband had a passion for golf, so the house would be occupied frequently during the year and the garden needed to look good at all times. She felt we could make her an informal-style garden, taking advantage of the very mild climate and exceptionally favourable growing conditions.

This was exciting as it meant we could use a host of Mediterranean-type plants, many of them quite outside our normal range. It has turned out to be a very challenging project and, as far as plants are concerned, a tough learning process. Plants cease to grow in the very hot summers. Growing actually takes place in the autumn and continues through the very mild winters, so preparations and planting are best done in the winter and spring. With an irrigation system, there is plenty of water (although, in a normal year, a very low rainfall).

The property is in the foothills of the mountains, along the coast from Gibraltar and only a few kilometres from the sea. Typical of the landscape are the beautiful cork oaks (*Quercus suber*), still in places grown commercially, where they make open woods that allow plenty of shrubby undergrowth. These oaks are only found naturally in siliceous soil (formed from the breakdown of rocks containing silica). From an horticultural point of view they thrive in sandy, very quick-draining soil, and adapt happily to garden conditions and to the irrigation systems which are essential in an area where a drought may last for several years. In this they differ from the American live oaks (*Q. virginiana* and *Q. agrifolia*) which react badly to irrigation, often developing root disease, and resent any sort of compaction. There seems to be no need for workmen in Spain to respect the cork oak and its roots.

Fortunately, there were some handsome old oaks growing among the native *maquis* on the new garden site and, after pruning and feeding, these and some wild olives are already important features. Before the site was cleared for building, native plants growing under the oaks included arbutus, tree heathers (*Erica arborea*), resinous pistacias (both the evergreen mastic tree, *P. lentiscus*, and the deciduous *P. terebinthus*), buckthorn, cistus, broom – all typical *maquis* plants with aromatic leaves which resist

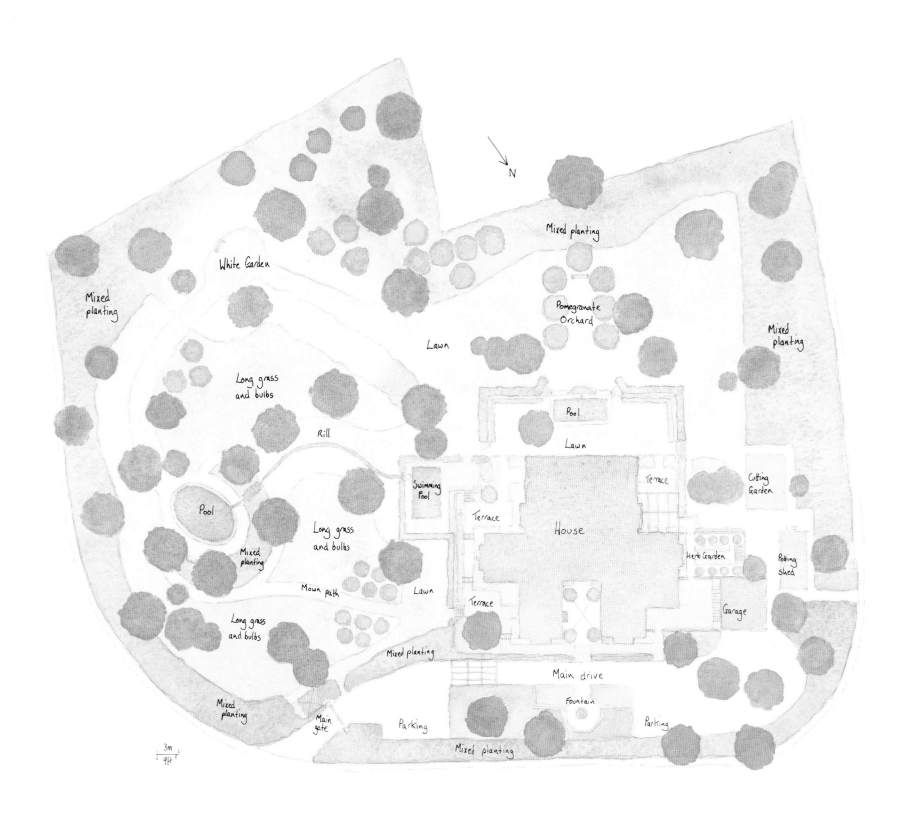

fierce sun and drought. As the house went up, we decided to replant a selection of evergreen natives round the perimeter of the garden so that the site would be screened from the road and would look relatively undisturbed. However, it is not always easy to get good specimens of local indigenous plants. Pistacias, for example, are virtually unknown in the nursery trade but they will regenerate from the roots and some are now coming back after the initial clearing. We have also added swathes of other Mediterranean-type plants: bay (*Laurus nobilis*) in quantity, laurustinus (*Viburnum tinus*) and phillyreas as evergreen screens; more olives, Judas trees (*Cercis siliquastrum*), carobs (*Ceratonia obliqua*), Jerusalem sage (*Phlomis fruticosa*), myrtles, rosemary and acanthus. In a year's time the house will be almost invisible from the road.

The new house, designed by a brilliant architect, Eduardo Dorissa Rosanes from Seville, is built in the typical Andalucian style, with shady loggias and tree-shaded terraces. When we first saw it under construction, isolated in a sea of mud, we knew we must give it a place in the landscape. Most of the garden, sloping away to the south-east and dominated by cork oaks, has been designed in a naturalistic style, planted with a mixture of suitable natives and exotics for all-year-round interest. Grass has been sown by experts from the golf course, using seed specially adapted for shade under the oak trees. Tightly mown pathways lead to open sunlit spaces where we hope to introduce many of the small native bulbs, such as narcissus and crocus (some endemic to the region), which are found growing naturally in more open sun-baked *garigue* but not in the *maquis* woodland. One path leads to a White Garden where roses, lemon-scented verbena, white *Vitex agnus-castus*, cistus, philadelphus and

agapanthus provide the mass of the planting.

A broad and sloping path between the cork oaks dropped into an clearing in the lower woodland and here we made an oval pool, fed by a water rill, to be planted with waterlilies and *Cyperus papyrus*. In spite of the lack of naturally moist soil, we are able, thanks to the effective irrigation system, to plant more richly in this dell, using large-leaved plants to achieve a tropical effect: red cannas, many different gingers, blue-flowered echiums, feijoas, *Melianthus major* and exotics such as *Beschorneria yuccoides* from Mexico, with fleshy strap leaves and arching flower stems. By spring 1997, this area will have developed a luxurious appearance.

The garden directly around the house is more sophisticated, with formal terraces, pools and fountains hedged with evergreens to make a series of interlocking horizontals. The hedges include Mediterranean myrtle (*Myrtus communis*), glossy-leaved *Eugenia myrtifolia* from Australia, and tall and short forms of Japanese pittosporum (*P. tobira* and *P. t.* 'Nana'), all with scented flowers in their season but glossy-leaved and healthy for the rest of the year. With the heat and watering system, growth here is very rapid and hedges will need frequent clipping.

On the terraces and round the pools by the house we have planted eclectically: grey-leaved *Westringia fruticosa* from Australia, with pale lavender flowers, daturas (now brugmansias), gingers, prostrate rosemarys, lavenders (*Lavandula stoechas* ssp. *pedunculata*), and blue and white agapanthus massed in various spots. A jacaranda shades part of the swimming pool terrace.

We have chosen many climbers to clothe both the house and the arches that link the terraces. The walls are washed a strong pinkish-red so we have avoided climbers that produce harsh yellow flowers. White wisteria

scrambles over the front loggia and up frames onto the roof. Evergreen *Trachelospermum jasminoides* with scented white flowers, white and blue plumbagos, pink mandevillas, *Thunbergia grandiflora* with violet-blue flowers, white scented jasmine and *Solanum jasminoides* 'Album', all curtain the house walls.

There is still much to do. All this planting, still in progress in winter 1996, has yet to settle and develop. Perennials and bulbs have to be added, especially for spring effects, and tender roses planted under the oaks have yet to clamber upwards and make a cascade of bloom. I hope to grow many different salvias, especially those from the New World which come from similar habitats. The garden will fill out in a few seasons (growth here is so spectacular) and already the house nestles happily amongst the cork oaks with the garden maturing around it.

OPPOSITE, TOP *The silvery-leaved evergreen* Melianthus major *from South Africa is grown for its striking architectural foliage.*

OPPOSITE, MIDDLE Solanum rantonnetii *(syn.* Lycianthes rantonnetii*), the blue potato vine from South America, is a lax shrub that needs support to grow upwards on the house walls.*

OPPOSITE, BELOW *The view up the steps and along the arch-covered walk that links two terraces on the southern side of the house.*

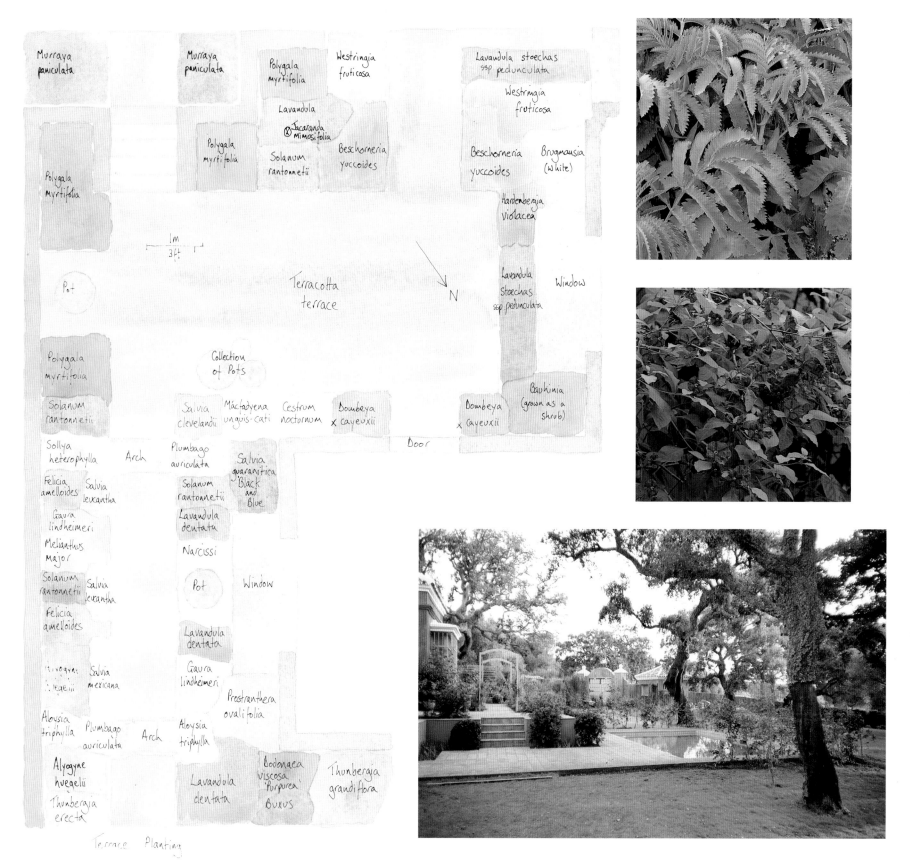

Murraya
paniculata

Murraya
paniculata

Polygala
myrtifolia

Westringia
fruticosa

Lavandula stoechas
ssp pedunculata

Westringia
fruticosa

Lavandula

⊗ Jacaranda
mimosifolia

Polygala
myrtifolia

Polygala
myrtifolia

Solanum
rantonnetii

Beschorneria
yuccoides

Beschorneria
yuccoides

Brugmansia
(white)

Hardenbergia
violacea

1m / 3ft

Pot

Terracotta
terrace

N

Lavandula
stoechas
ssp pedunculata

Window

Polygala
myrtifolia

Collection
of Pots

Baukinia
(grown as a
shrub)

Solanum
rantonnetii

Salvia
clevelandii

Macfadyena
unguis-cati

Cestrum
nocturnum

Dombeya
x Cayeuxii

Dombeya
x Cayeuxii

Sollya
heterophylla

Arch

Plumbago
auriculata

Door

Felicia
amelloides

Salvia
leucantha

Solanum
rantonnetii

Salvia
guaranitica
'Black
and
Blue'

Gaura
lindheimeri

Lavandula
dentata

Melianthus
major

Narcissi

Solanum
rantonnetii

Salvia
leucantha

Pot

Window

Felicia
amelloides

Lavandula
dentata

Hibiscus
huegelii

Salvia
mexicana

Gaura
lindheimeri

Prostranthera
ovalifolia

Aloysia
triphylla

Plumbago
auriculata

Arch

Aloysia
triphylla

Alyogyne
huegelii

Lavandula
dentata

Dodonaea
viscosa
'Purpurea'

Thunbergia
grandiflora

Thunbergia
erecta

Buxus

Terrace Planting

147

FORMALITY AND PROFUSION IN MY OWN GARDEN

OPPOSITE *The Dorset hills make a splendid backdrop to views of the garden to the north and west. The high-walled inner garden is on two levels, and in the central lower part my new Gravel Garden has replaced the lawn, with crosspaths meeting at the centre at a small square pool edged with French limestone. From here, the view draws the eye through the glass doors into the outer garden on the other side of the house.*

We bought our house at Bettiscombe – a ruined Coach House – for its unique situation looking out over the Dorset landscape, and for the existing walled garden tucked behind it. By the time I moved there from Tintinhull in 1993 my husband, John Malins, was dead, but we had made plans together for the empty garden canvas, almost .4ha (1 acre) in extent. On the north side of the house the meadow, on the shoulder of the hill with a backdrop of high downland, was to become an orchard, allowing the landscape a dominant presence without intrusive exotic trees. Semi-domestic crabs, mulberries, old varieties of apple (a gift from the gardener from my old college, Girton at Cambridge) seemed appropriate choices. The inner walled garden to the south, almost a square, was to be quite formal, with paths parallel and at right angles to the wall, allowing axes and cross vistas, a central lawn and flower-beds. The Tintinhull influence would be strong here.

By the time the house was habitable, we had transformed the sloping inner garden into two levels, connected by three sets of shallow steps made from old kerb stones, the banks between them planted with sprawling roses and perennials. We had also developed the most important view, by having glass doors made on either side of the house to carry the eye in both directions to an avenue of yew – to be clipped as topiary pyramids or pillars. This repetition in the inner and outer gardens linked the high-walled *hortus conclusus* with the orchard and the landscape. The pathways were laid using local hoggin – compressed gravel dressed and bound with clay dust.

At ground level the bones of the garden were set and I was now faced with the vital task of converting the difficult soil into viable loam before starting detailed planting. The soil at Bettiscombe is very heavy clay, waterlogged in winter and drying out into cement-like blocks in summer. We had already used weedkiller to eliminate mare's-tail and Japanese knotweed but I needed lots of help to improve soil structure. My stalwart day-and-a-half-a-week gardener, Brian Gray, has done all the digging and mulching. We imported some topsoil and double-dug all the beds three or four times, incorporating mushroom compost (which contains gypsum, a clay-breaker) and grit. Since this initial preparation we no longer dig but add handfuls of 6mm (¼in) grit whenever we plant. All the beds are mulched at least once a year; I like to do this in both autumn and early summer, if possible.

Planting throughout the garden has been designed to make less work in the years to come, to ease my gardening old age. Bettiscombe, although 75m (250ft) above sea level, is far enough south-west and near

ABOVE *The view to the north through the glass doors, looking across the meadow lined with yew pillars to the downland beyond.*

enough to the English Channel to allow experiments with tender specimens that were impossible in the much colder Tintinhull garden. I included plenty of spring- and summer-flowering shrubs in my plans, especially the tender evergreens that I love; eventually they will leave little space for flowering perennials, and the only late-season colour will be supplied by many small-flowered Viticella-type clematis scrambling through them.

On the upper level I used structural plants to fill cubic space and to help divide the garden into rooms for different themes and

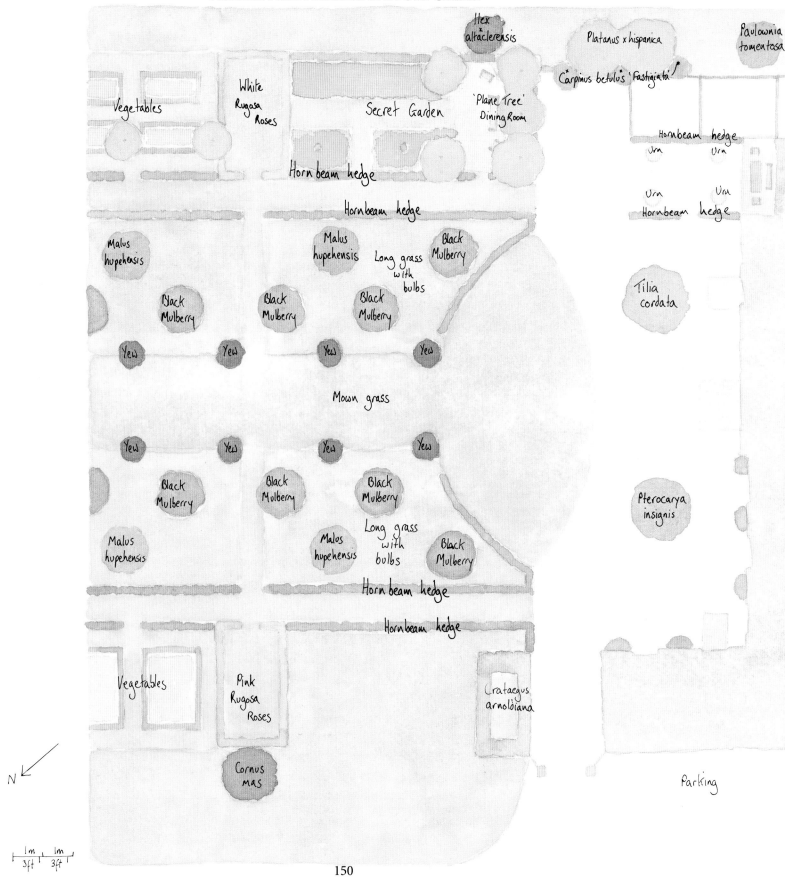

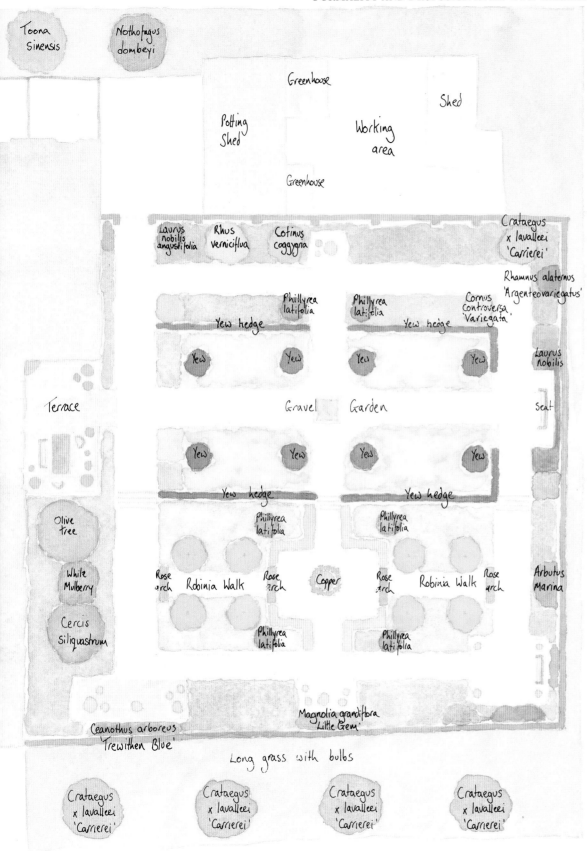

Toona
sinensis

Nothofagus
dombeyi

Greenhouse

Potting
Shed

Working
area

Shed

Greenhouse

Laurus
nobilis
angustifolia

Rhus
verniciflua

Cotinus
coggygria

Crataegus
x lavalleei
'Carrierei'

Rhamnus alaternus
'Argenteovariegatus'

Phillyrea
latifolia

Phillyrea
latifolia

Cornus
controversa
Variegata'

Yew hedge

Yew hedge

Laurus
Nobilis

Terrace

Yew

Yew

Yew

Yew

Gravel   Garden

Seat

Yew

Yew

Yew

Yew

Yew hedge

Yew hedge

Olive
tree

Phillyrea
latifolia

Phillyrea
latifolia

White
Mulberry

Rose
arch

Robinia Walk

Rose
arch

Copper

Rose
arch

Robinia Walk

Rose
arch

Arbutus
Marina

Cercis
siliquastrum

Phillyrea
latifolia

Phillyrea
latifolia

Ceanothus arboreus
'Trewithen Blue'

Magnolia grandiflora
'Little Gem'

Long grass with bulbs

Crataegus
x lavalleei
'Carrierei'

Crataegus
x lavalleei
'Carrierei'

Crataegus
x lavalleei
'Carrierei'

Crataegus
x lavalleei
'Carrierei'

Blue ceanothus is intertwined with Clematis 'Bill MacKenzie' on the upper wall of the garden.

A double white Rosa banksiae grows in an upturned rhubarb forcer on the south-facing wall of the house.

colours, with spreading alchemilla, cranesbills, hellebores in shade, hollyhocks, polemoniums and bronze fennel interspersed with stands of *Crambe cordifolia* to ensure that there is plenty of flowering interest. Eight globe locusts (*Robinia pseudoacacia* 'Umbraculifera') and four *Phillyrea latifolia* pillars provide plant architecture, and metal rose arches – for rambling roses and late-flowering clematis – frame views along a central path. The high walls are planted with wall shrubs and climbers, mostly spring-flowering shrubs with more summer- and late-flowering clematis to spread the seasons. Today, after three gardening seasons, spring ceanothus are intertwined with clematis, and a white banksian rose (*Rosa banksiae*), climbing hydrangeas (both the familiar

H. anomala petiolaris and *H. seemannii*), schizophragma, stauntonia and holboellias, blue and white potato flowers (*Solanum crispum* 'Glasnevin' and *S. jasminoides* 'Album') clothe the walls. In the beds are coronillas, *Drimys winteri, Itea ilicifolia*, the relatively new *Heptacodium jasminoides* from the Arnold Arboretum, and various olearias – a genus I love to collect. A specimen *Magnolia delavayi* has survived two winters but has yet to flower. Philadelphus and a few shrub roses add their scent in June and July. Smaller plants – shrubs, perennials and bulbs – include lavenders, rosemaries, a host of phlomis (many brought back from Greece as cuttings), alliums, summer-flowering agapanthus, and a selection of blue salvias grown annually from seed or cuttings.

Although there is little self-conscious colour-scheming, one wall bed is predominantly 'blue', with central beds in dusty pinks with glaucous and purple foliage, and another is mainly 'white'.

On the lower level a central lawn was planted with eight yew pillars and lined with yew hedges, planted only 30cm (12in) high but planned to be clipped at just over 1m (3ft 6in). I planted a broad-headed hawthorn (*Crataegus* x *lavalleei* 'Carrierei') and a giant dogwood (*Cornus controversa* 'Variegata'), its green leaves on tabulated branches edged with white, and two more phillyrea to be encouraged to grow into tree shape, with a smoke bush (*Cotinus coggygria*) and varnish tree (*Rhus verniciflua*) to disguise the roofs of the garden sheds and give some privacy.

In 1995, after a drought during which the grass almost died out, I decided to get rid of the central lawn. We have a limited water supply from a neighbour, and never enough for plants and the many pots. I wanted to create a Gravel Garden in which some shrubs would give structure around the existing yews, but where the rest of the planting would be of Mediterranean-type plants, many of which would self-seed and form spreading naturalistic groups. I had been inspired in this by Beth Chatto's new gravel garden in Essex and by John Brookes's approach at Denmans in Sussex. However, both the design ideas and the conditions were very different at Bettiscombe. Although planned to look as natural as possible, my design had to fit in with the existing

OPPOSITE *A view across the garden shows the architectural globe locusts filling the cubic space on the upper level. In the Gravel Garden the yew hedges and pillars are just visible. It will be several years before they fulfil their function of tying this new area into the overall design.*

RIGHT *The strange, hooded blue-purple flowers of the Greek* Cerinthe major *'Purpurascens', grown from seed, with the tall biennial Scotch thistle (*Onopordum acanthium*), with variegated* Iris pallida *subsp.* pallida *and the Siberian catmint* Nepeta sibirica *'Souvenir d'André Chaudron'.*

OVERLEAF *A copper pot planted with blue lyme grass (*Leymus arenarius*) and* Parahebe perfoliata *is buttressed with alternating Jerusalem sage and rosemary. Set in a sea of* Nepeta *'Six Hills Giant' and with roses and clematis on arches either side, it makes a feature on the upper level.*

153

OPPOSITE *A new area in the outer garden, eventually to consist of a garden of white Rugosa roses, is planted with purple-leaved orach, opium poppies, nasturtiums and red dahlias. The raised vegetable beds are seen in the distance. Hornbeam hedges will soon conceal the hidden gardens within.*

BELOW *A pair of airy* Stipa gigantea *rise out of a sea of catmint to flank the top of the central steps. In autumn, long after other flowers are over, grasses will continue to shine, highlighted by the low winter sun.*

BELOW RIGHT *Pots on a small paved area in the upper garden are planted with salvias, trailing* Convolvulus sabatius *and* Verbena bonariensis. *I change the planting each season but most of the flowers under the wall are blue through the summer season, so I keep these pots for the many salvias I grow on from seed or cuttings each year.*

formality of the garden structure. This meant that I would need to keep axes and cross vistas and include vertical plants and repetitive shapes and colours.

The soil needed very thorough preparation to provide the drainage essential for 'silvers' and self-seeders. Whereas in the rest of the garden I grow plants that will acclimatize to the existing site, in the Gravel Garden I am creating artificial conditions for the plants I want. We put in additional drainage, brought in topsoil and incorporated gravel while deep digging; we also used the gravel as a mulch. The beds are, in fact, like large planters, while the paths, barely distinguishable from the prepared flowerbeds, have a 3cm (just over 1in) layer of topsoil under the gravel to help the seeders.

Undulating plant shapes edge the pathways, while verbascums, grey-leaved thistles (onopordums and *Galactites*

tomentosa, all with long tap-roots), *Salvia* 'Indigo Spires', *S. patens* and seeders such as *S. sclarea* var. *turkestanica* are more vertical. *Nicotiana glauca* and other tobaccos including *N. langsdorffii*, *N. rustica* and *N. sylvestris*, with plenty of Russian sage (*Perovskia atriplicifolia*) are planted in groups. In 1996 three groups of cerinthe, mainly *Cerinthe major* 'Purpurascens', grown from seed brought home from Greece the previous spring, were eye-catchers. Seeders include salvias, erodiums, opium and Welsh poppies, Texas blue-bonnets and *Glaucium flavum*; these will all need strict editing every spring. The yew pillars, standard Russian olives (*Elaeagnus angustifolia*) and other shrubs, including *Acer palmatum* 'Senkaki' and *A. pensylvanicum* 'Erythrocladum', both with interesting pink bark in winter, a golden-leaved catalpa, olearias and philadelphus provide all-year-round interest.

To the east of the Gravel Garden, the pair of borders stretching below the south-east walls and aligned on the church tower and my bedroom window, are mainly filled with golden foliage plants but will ultimately be dominated by the dogwood underplanted with hostas. A collection of euphorbias, woad (*Isatis tinctoria*) and seeding *Smyrnium perfoliatum* all have acid-yellow flowers but are given a taste of blue with the spreading summer-flowering goat's rue (*Galega orientalis*) from the Caucasus, which, cut back after flowering, will produce fresh green foliage in late summer.

The outer garden, planned as an orchard, has had embellishments. Yews, black mulberries (*Morus nigra*) and crab apples (*Malus hupehensis*) grow in meadow grass dotted with spring bulbs, lining a central mown axis aligned on a large (empty) pot, a *lemonaiao*. Two alleys and an outer line, all of hornbeam, create an almost square central area – roughly approximate in size to the inner walled garden. Beyond the hornbeam there are further garden areas which will, as the hedges mature, be screened from view from the house. At either side, raised beds grow vegetables, and caged enclosures, curtained with blue sweet peas in summer, are for compost. A small secret garden, overlooked by a shady plane tree sitting area, is planted with white Rugosa roses, red dahlias and chocolate-scented cosmos.

Many of the new trees, shrubs and climbers contribute red, golden and yellow autumn foliage which, in the inner garden, is enhanced by vivid late-flowering kniphofias and bright blue aconitums, and, in the outer garden, by scarlet dahlias and bright Rugosa hips. In the meadow, the mulberries turn a soft, almost translucent, yellow in October. But throughout the summer the predominantly green and gold of grasses in the meadow and the backdrop of brown, buff, green and gold in the fields and hills beyond contrast with the colour and bustle of the inner garden, bringing welcome relief. This is where I like to be in the evening light. Bettiscombe has given me a chance to design for myself with strong structured outlines, but also to return to my original passion for plants. I believe it is possible to combine classic principles with the collector's urge to have a very wide selection.

PROPOSAL FOR A ROYAL GARDEN

BELOW *The site of the new garden – a large sweep of lawn, a few Irish yews and an Edwardian tennis hut flanked by herbaceous borders – with Walmer Castle and the sea beyond.*

ABOVE *From the designs proposed by Sir Anthony Denny, Her Majesty chose this stone* loggia *to replace the old tennis hut.*

In October 1995 we received a letter from English Heritage, inviting us to take part in a competition to design a new garden in the grounds of Walmer Castle in Kent. The Castle, now under the stewardship of English Heritage, is the official residence of the Lord Warden of the Cinque Ports, a position held since 1978 by Her Majesty Queen Elizabeth the Queen Mother. English Heritage had decided to celebrate Her Majesty's ninety-fifth birthday, and her tenure as Lord Warden, with the present of a garden in her honour. We were flattered by the invitation and delighted to accept the challenge.

The Cinque Ports – originally Sandwich, Dover, Hastings, Hythe and Romney, but later increased in number – formed an ancient federation which, in the days before a Royal Navy, provided the Sovereign with ships in return for a wide range of privileges and local jurisdiction. The Lord Wardenship of the Cinque Ports lies within the gift of the Monarch, and has traditionally been the reward for political or military success: past Wardens have included Pitt the Younger, the Duke of Wellington (who died in Walmer Castle), and Sir Winston Churchill. The Queen Mother is the first woman to hold the post. However, the Lord Warden was usually also Constable of Dover Castle, and Walmer did not become the official residence until the tenure of the Duke of Dorset in the early eighteenth century.

Walmer Castle was built by Henry VIII in 1539 as one of a chain of forts to protect against the threat of invasion. It stands directly on the sea shore, looking across the English Channel to France. By the time of its construction, military technology had rendered traditional castle architecture virtually obsolete. Walmer, with its sister castles at Deal and Sandown, was designed rather as a fortified gun emplacement; there are no straight lines, only curves that would deflect a cannon ball. The form of the Castle, a Tudor rose, is no design whimsy but a fine example of the old maxim of function dictating form.

Over the centuries, various Lords Warden have left their mark on the Castle gardens. William Pitt's niece, Lady Hester Stanhope, helped with the original layout of the garden as it is today, but it was Earl Granville (Lord Warden 1865-91) who put down the double line of yew hedges and generous borders that flank the gravel walk to the west of the Castle. Earl Beauchamp introduced several tennis courts in the early twentieth century.

To the south of the Castle, enclosed on three sides by high brick walls and on two sides by mature sycamores, lay the site of the proposed new garden. For two centuries it had been successively a kitchen garden, rose garden, tennis court and orchard, but when we first saw it, contained little more than a large lawn, an Edwardian tennis hut, and a

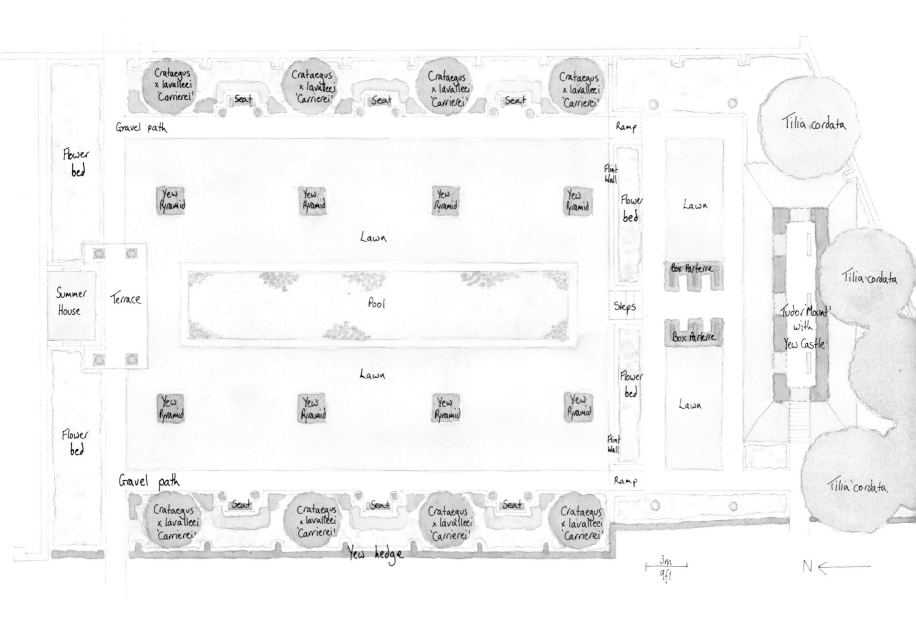

Crataegus
x lavallleei
'Carrierei'

Seat

Crataegus
x lavallleei
'Carrierei'

Seat

Crataegus
x lavallleei
'Carrierei'

Seat

Crataegus
x lavallleei
'Carrierei'

Gravel path

Ramp

Flower
bed

Flint
Wall

Flower
bed

Lawn

Tilia cordata

Yew
Pyramid

Yew
Pyramid

Yew
Pyramid

Yew
Pyramid

Lawn

Box Parterre

Summer
House

Terrace

Pool

Steps

Box Parterre

Tudor 'Mount'
with
Yew Castle

Tilia cordata

Lawn

Flower
bed

Lawn

Yew
Pyramid

Yew
Pyramid

Yew
Pyramid

Yew
Pyramid

Flower
bed

Flint
Wall

Tilia cordata

Gravel path

Ramp

Crataegus
x lavallleei
'Carrierei'

Seat

Crataegus
x lavallleei
'Carrierei'

Seat

Crataegus
x lavallleei
'Carrierei'

Seat

Crataegus
x lavallleei
'Carrierei'

Tilia cordata

Yew hedge

3m
9ft

N

Section through
middle of garden

few Irish yews. Our brief from English Heritage was very specific: to use the whole space, approximately half an acre (.2ha); to incorporate the existing change of level; to highlight views of the Castle; to screen houses that lay beyond the garden walls; and to take full advantage of the mild maritime climate. We could expect the garden to be tended for up to three full days a week. Our budget was fair but not extravagant.

We were acutely aware that our work needed to be especially sensitive to place and person: not only were we designing in an ancient and important site, but the garden was to be a royal one.

We sat in the tennis hut, in the low October sunlight, looking out into the empty green space and trying to imagine what Her Majesty might most like to see. Swallows, winging low over water, was an image that came to mind: a central canal, 30m (95ft) long in honour of her birthday, could give the garden a strong line. Her Majesty's childhood home, St Paul's Walden Bury, with its French baroque influence, inspired formal gardens on either side of the canal. Four clipped yew pyramids on the lawns would be matched by round-headed trees (we chose hybrid thorns for their glossy foliage and autumn berries) with a simple underplanting of *Vinca difformis* with *Lilium martagon* 'Album' and *Leucojum aestivum*. We could

replace the tennis hut with a more elegant structure.

The views along the garden to the houses beyond presented a particular problem. One house looms over the Castle walls; hiding it would be difficult. However, we could use the spoil from digging the canal to create an earthwork reminiscent of a Tudor Mount. On top of the Mount a folly could go, a yew castle 4m (13ft) high from whose clipped arches one could look back over the garden to the Castle itself. At its base, two topiary 'E's could 'anchor' the mound and offer their own historical associations. As further concealment, an existing group of small-leaved lime (*Tilia cordata*) that stood beyond

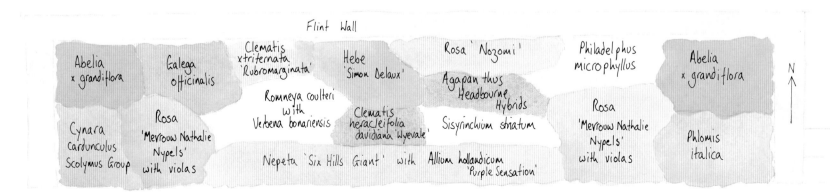

Flint Wall Flower Beds

the immediate garden boundary would be extended and wrapped around the flanks of the Mount.

With the bare bones of the layout roughed out, it was time to look at details. The building materials should echo those already used in the Castle gardens – local gravel, knapped flint and red brick for walls. For the terraces, caps to walls and copings for the pool, Caithness stone from Sutherland was chosen. To bring stone from Scotland to the coast of Kent might seem strange but Her Majesty's Castle of May, another castle by the sea and lovingly restored under her supervision, lies right on the northern tip of Sutherland. Stone from near this castle

would resonate in the garden at Walmer.

Lead planters embossed with Her Majesty's coat-of-arms and those of the Cinque Ports would be commissioned to furnish the summerhouse terrace.

The garden is to be open throughout the year but is designed to be at its best in July, when Her Majesty is in residence. Our plan included four south-facing borders – two either side of the summerhouse and a pair of narrower beds below the flint retaining wall. These could be filled with tender shrubs and perennials. Roses, much loved by Her Majesty, would interweave with philadelphus, regal lilies and clematis, while Californian poppies (*Romneya coulteri*),

Melianthus major and salvias would provide seasonal highlights.

Our outline plans were submitted to English Heritage in December 1995, and in the spring came the welcome news that our design had been selected. Through the autumn and winter of 1996, contractors have been hard at work translating our vision into a reality – laying paths and digging canals; clipping yew into pyramids and castle; forming box in a double 'E' pattern ready for transplanting; and assembling plants from nurseries throughout the land. By July 1997 the work should be complete, and Walmer Castle will give a very public present to its much-loved Warden.

Index

Page numbers in *italic type* denote references to photographs, plans and their captions.

HARDINESS ZONES
Approximate range of average annual minimum temperatures:

°CELSIUS	ZONES	°FAHRENHEIT
below -45	1	below -50
-45 to -40	2	-50 to -40
-40 to -34	3	-40 to -30
-34 to -29	4	-30 to -20
-29 to -23	5	-20 to -10
-23 to -18	6	-10 to 0
-18 to -12	7	0 to 10
-12 to -7	8	10 to 20
-7 to 1	9	20 to 30
-1 to 4	10	30 to 40
above 4	11	above 40

Hardiness zone ratings suggest the approximate minimum temperature plants will tolerate in winter. However, this can only be a rough guide. The hardiness of a plant depends on a great many factors, including the depths of its roots, its water content at the onset of frost, the duration of cold weather, the force of the wind, and the length and heat of the preceding summer. The zone ratings are based on those devised by the United States Department of Agriculture.

ACKNOWLEDGMENTS

Author's acknowledgments

My gratitude goes to all the wonderful owners who have made this book possible. I would like to thank them for asking us to help with their gardens and for allowing us to publish the results in this book. Working on their gardens has been interesting, rewarding and stimulating. It has been ten years of constant learning.

I am indebted to Simon Johnson, who works with me, for his help and cooperation.

My admiration and grateful thanks go to Andrew Lawson who took almost all the photographs in the UK for the book, and travelled to Italy, France and the USA, and to Jerry Harpur, Vivian Russell, Mick Hales, Erika Shank, Tony Lord, Cary Hazlegrove and Robert Polidori. Piers and Luke Simon, who have done the drawings and watercolours, rival the photographers with their talents.

As always, I owe an enormous debt of gratitude to Frances Lincoln and all her team: Erica Hunningher, Caroline Hillier, Sarah Mitchell, Trish Going, Anne Fraser and Caroline Taylor. Frances herself is always a watchful and encouraging presence. It is a privilege to be published by Frances Lincoln, and I am very proud of this.

Publishers' acknowledgments

Frances Lincoln Limited are grateful to all the garden owners, some of whom have chosen to remain anonymous, for permission to feature their gardens: English Heritage (pages 158-61 reproduced with the kind permission of English Heritage), Mr and Mrs Nicholas Horton-Fawkes, Gillian Lynne and Peter Land, Mr and Mrs Donald Macpherson, Simona and Vittorio Marzotto, The New York Botanical Garden in the Bronx, Richard O'Connell, Lord and Lady Pilkington, Julie and Stephen Riley, Jil Sander, Gabrielle and Alex Sheshunoff, Baron Sweerts de Landas Wyborgh (Sweerts de Landas Antique Garden Ornament, Dunsborough Park, Ripley, Woking, Surrey GU23 6AL, England; telephone 01483 225366), and Mr and Mrs William S. Taubman.

The Publishers also wish to offer special thanks to everyone who made the photography possible and to Antonia Johnson, Jo Christian, Anna Scott, James Bennett and Jon Folland for their help in producing this book.

Horticultural Consultant: Tony Lord
Watercolours: Piers Simon and Luke Simon
Plans annotation: Simon Johnson
Typesetting: Jon Anderson
Project Editor: Sarah Mitchell
Art Editor: Trish Going
Picture Editor: Anne Fraser
Editor: Caroline Taylor
Indexer: Penny David
Production: Jennifer Cohen, Peter Hinton
Design assistance: Caroline Clark

Editorial Director: Erica Hunningher
Art Director: Caroline Hillier
Production Director: Nicky Bowden

BELOW *In the warm walled garden at Bettiscombe in Dorset, the terrace makes an inviting area for sitting. Both tender* Alyogyne huegelii *'Santa Cruz' from south western Australia with blue mallow-like flowers and the dark-leaved* Eucomis *'Zeal Bronze' in the pots on the wall are wintered under glass.*

Photographic acknowledgments

a: above c: centre b: below r: right l: left

Mick Hales: 73-76, 79-80

Jerry Harpur: 2/3, 9, 13-17, 44-51, 66-68a, 69a, 70-71

Cary Hazlegrove: 77a

Penelope Hobhouse: 41a, 68b, 69b

Andrew Lawson: 1, 4-7, 10-12, 18-37a, 38-39, 41b-43, 52-65, 77c, 77 b, 82-99, 118-132, 137b, 147ar, 147al, 148-157, 168

Tony Lord: 37c, 37b

Robert Polidori: 81

Vivian Russell: 100-108a, 109-111, 134-137a

Erika Shank: 108b, 112-116, 138-143

Piers Simon: 144, 147b

Steven Wooster: 158a (with kind permission of English Heritage)